EASY PIANO

ULTIMATE

CHRISTMAS

3rd EDITION

W9-BUU-954

♦ 100 SEASONAL FAVORITES ♦

ISBN 978-0-7935-0944-7

HAL•LEONARD®
CORPORATION
7777 W. BLUEMOUND RD. P.O. BOX 13819 MILWAUKEE, WI 53213

Visit Hal Leonard Online at
www.halleonard.com

EASY PIANO

ULTIMATE

CHRISTMAS

• 100 SEASONAL FAVORITES •

CAROL OF THE BELLS

Ukrainian Christmas Carol

Exuberantly (𝅗𝅥. = 1 beat)

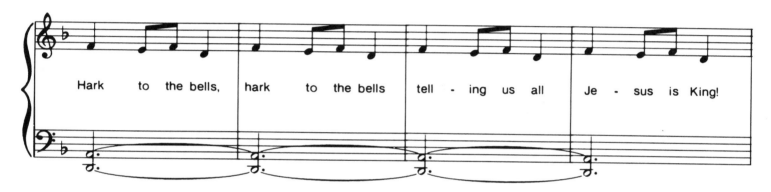

Hark to the bells, hark to the bells tell - ing us all Je - sus is King!

Strong - ly they chime, sound with a rhyme, Christ - mas is here!

Wel - come the King! Hark to the bells, hark to the bells,

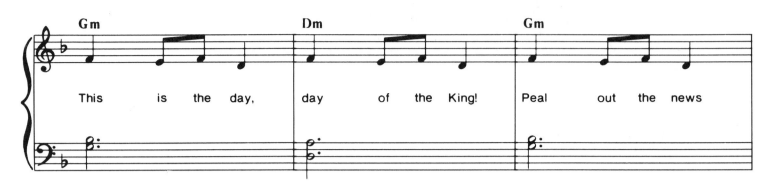

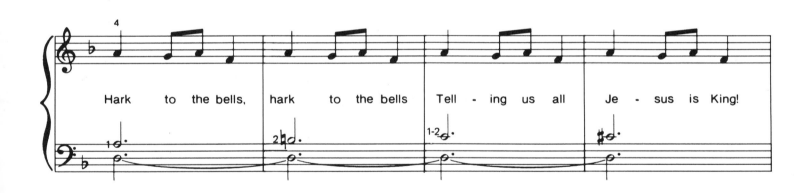

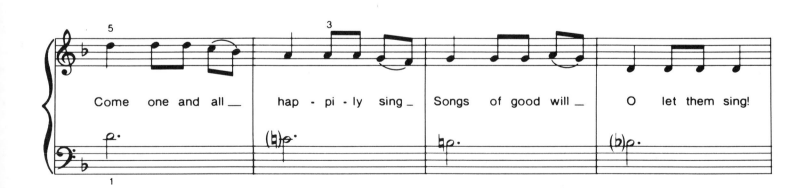

11

ANGELS WE HAVE HEARD ON HIGH

Traditional French Carol
Translated by JAMES CHADWICK

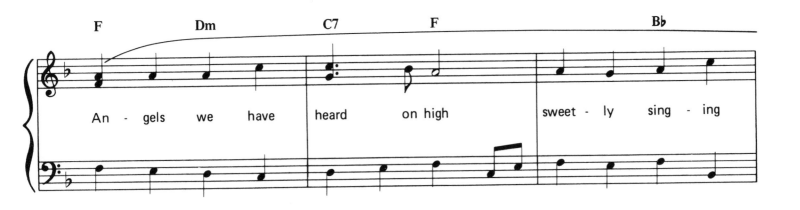

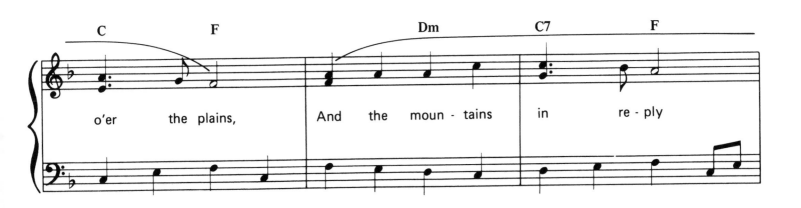

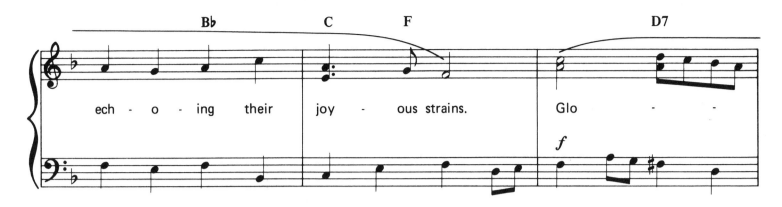

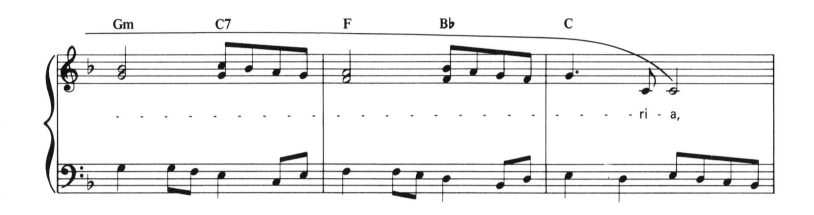

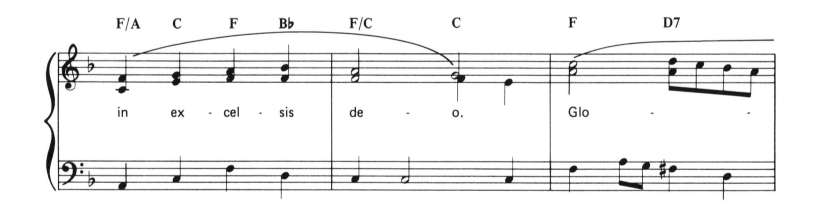

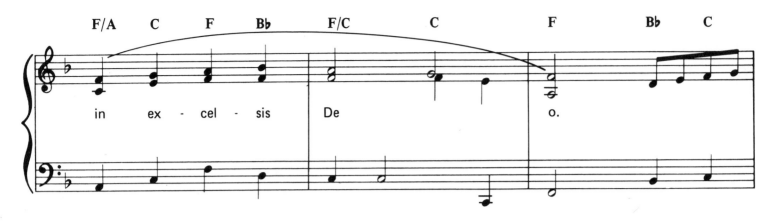

in ex - cel - sis De o.

Shep - herds why this ju - bi - lee, why your joy - ous

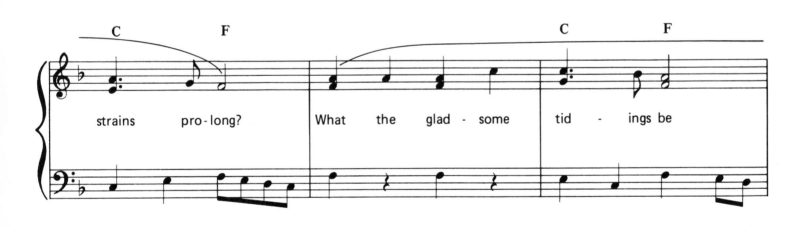

strains pro - long? What the glad - some tid - ings be

which in - spire your heaven - ly song? Glo

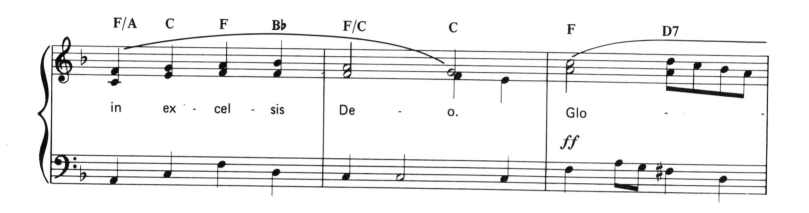

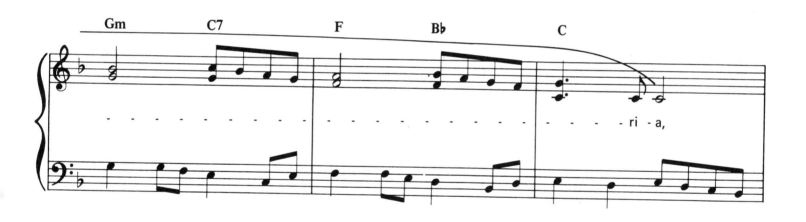

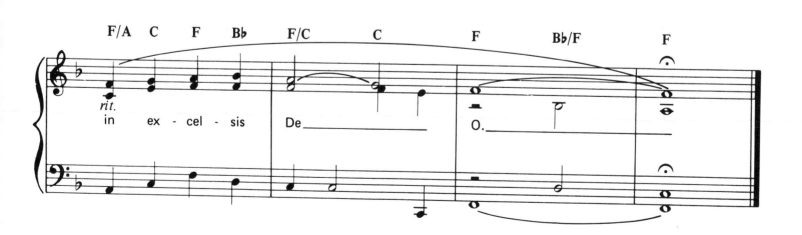

AULD LANG SYNE

Words by ROBERT BURNS
Traditional Scottish Melody

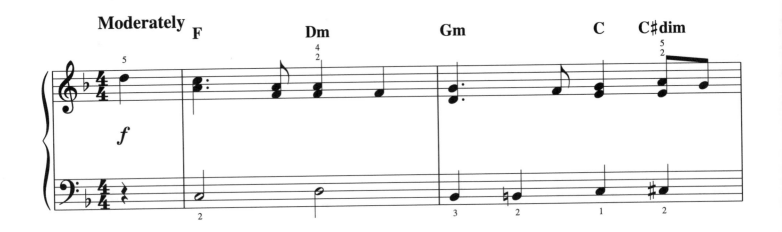

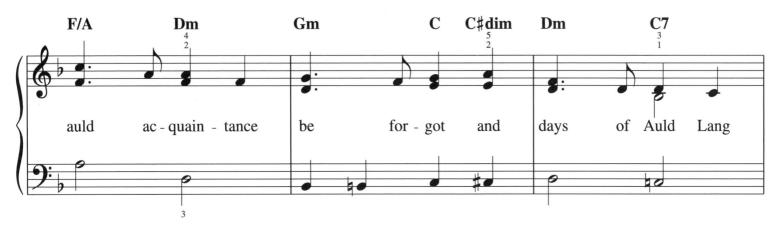

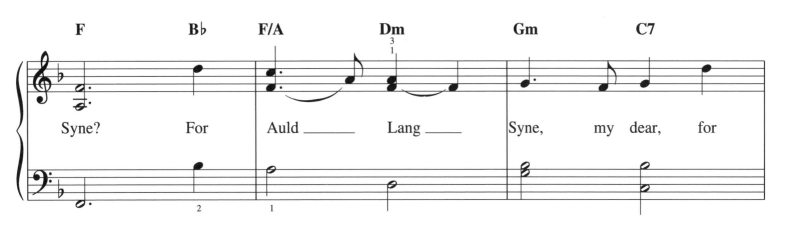

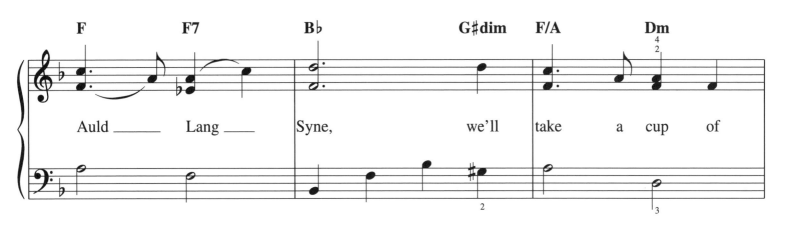

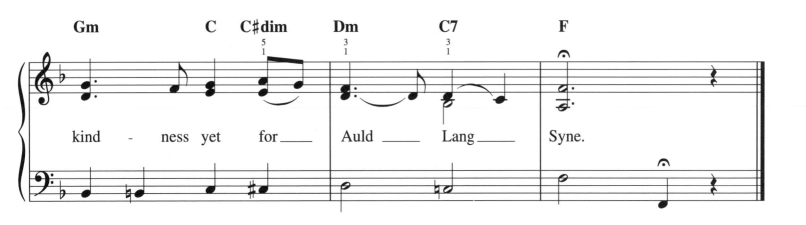

AWAY IN A MANGER

Traditional
Words by JOHN T. McFARLAND (v.3)
Music by JAMES R. MURRAY

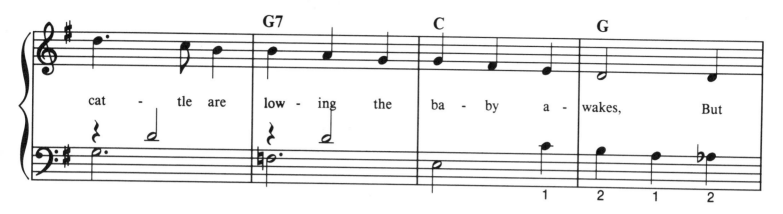

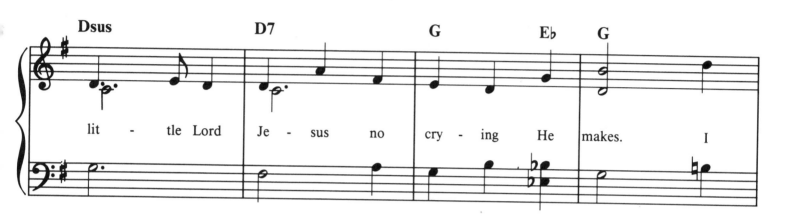

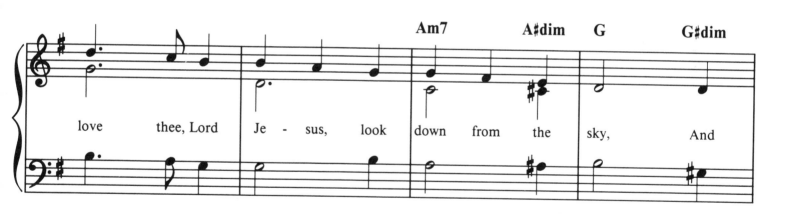

20

AWAY IN A MANGER

Anonymous Text (vv.1,2)
Text by JOHN T. McFARLAND (v.3)
Music by JONATHAN E. SPILLMAN

21

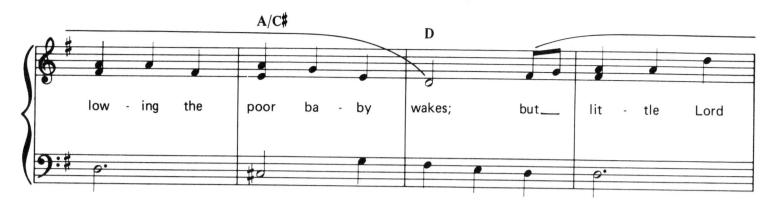

low - ing the poor ba - by wakes; but__ lit - tle Lord

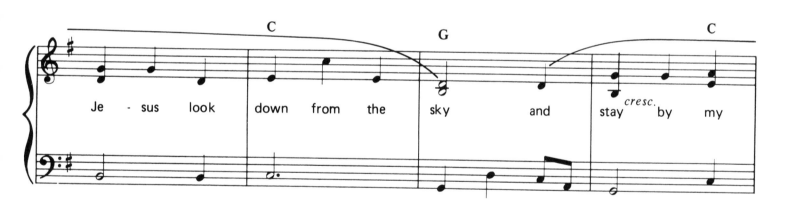

Je - sus no cry - ing__ He__ makes. I love thee Lord__

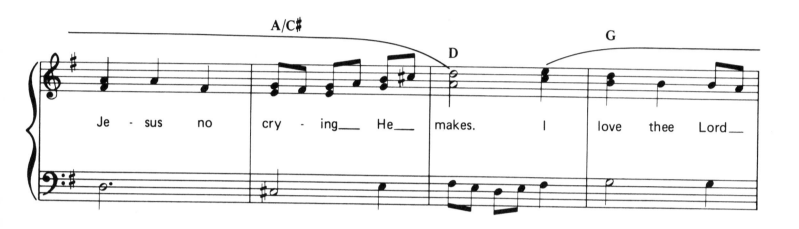

Je - sus look down from the sky and stay *cresc.* by my

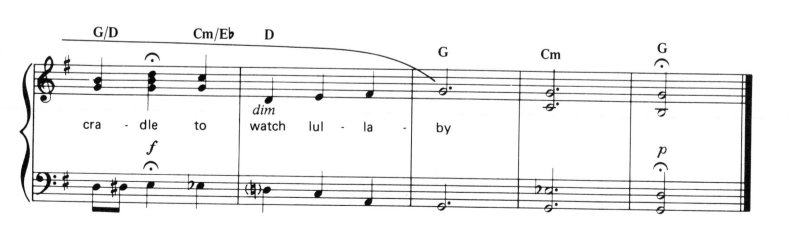

cra - dle to watch lul - la - by

BRING A TORCH, JEANNETTE, ISABELLA

17th Century French Provençal Carol

Flowing

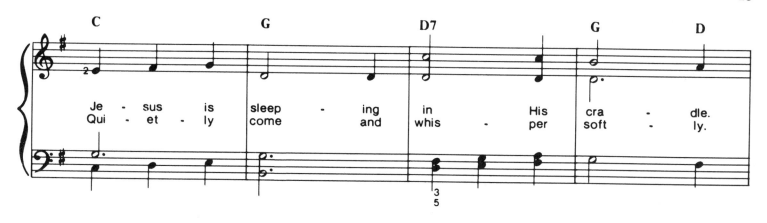

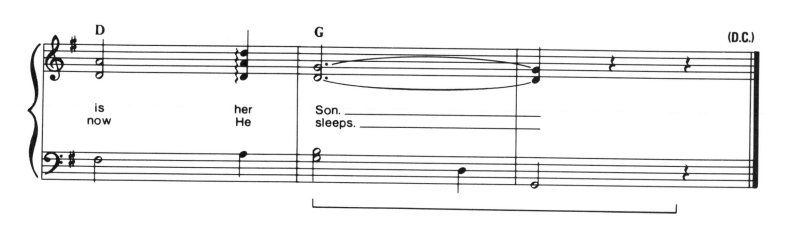

CAROLING, CAROLING

Words by WIHLA HUTSON
Music by ALFRED BURT

With a Lilt

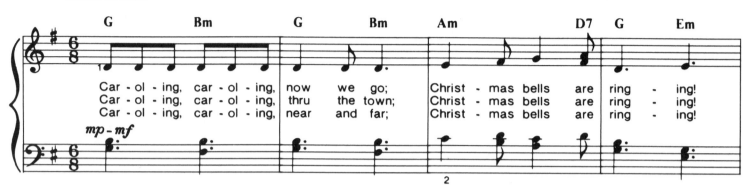

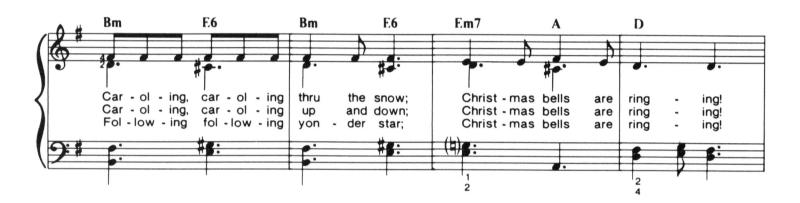

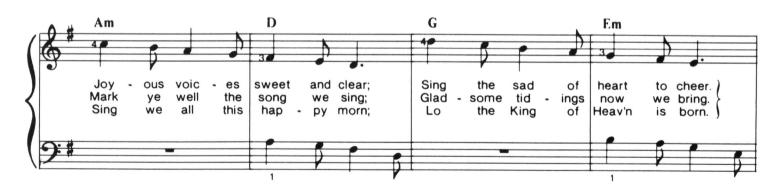

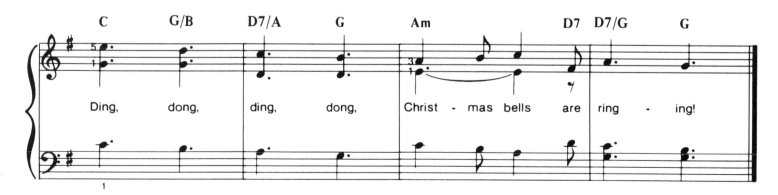

CHRIST WAS BORN ON CHRISTMAS DAY

Traditional

Moderately Bright

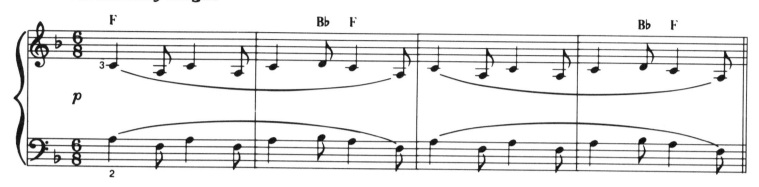

Christ was born on Christ - mas day, Wreath the hol - ly, twine the bay

Christ - us na - tus ho - di - e The Babe, the Son, the Ho - ly One of Ma - ry.

2. He is born to set us free,
He is born our Lord to be,
Ex Maria Virgine;
The God, The Lord, by all adored forever.

3. Let the bright red berries glow,
Everywhere in goodly show;
Christus natus hodie;
The Babe, the Son, the Holy One of Mary.

4. Christian men rejoice and sing,
'Tis the birthday of a King,
Ex Maria Virgine;
The God, the Lord, by all adored forever.

THE CHIPMUNK SONG

Words and Music by
ROSS BAGDASARIAN

Both hands may be played one octave higher than written.

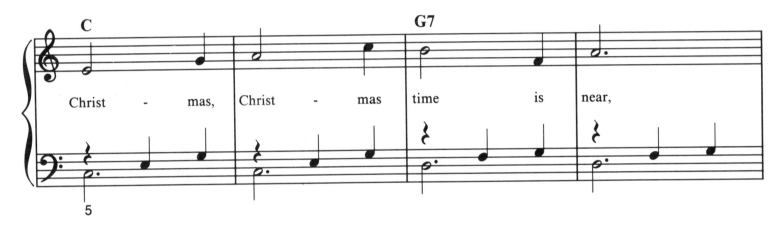

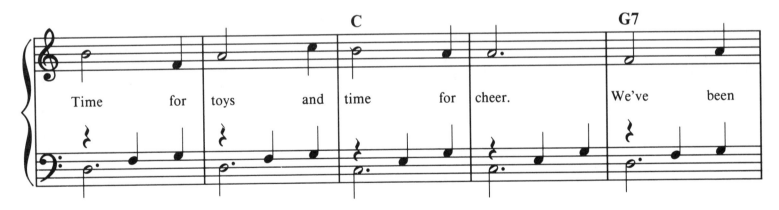

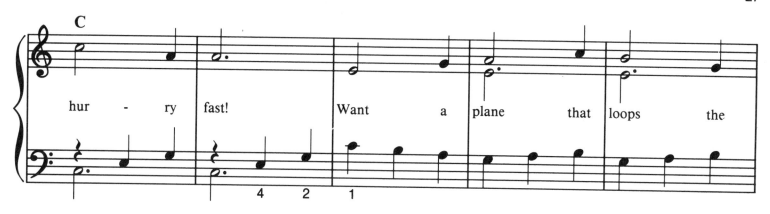

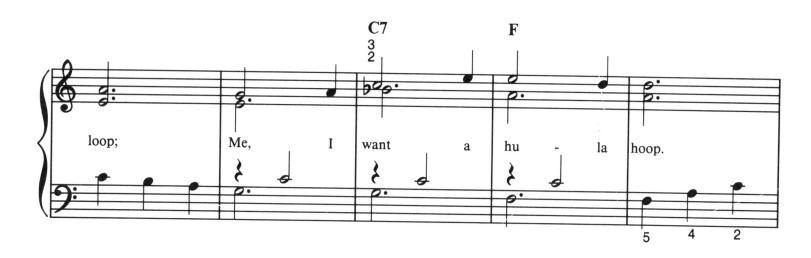

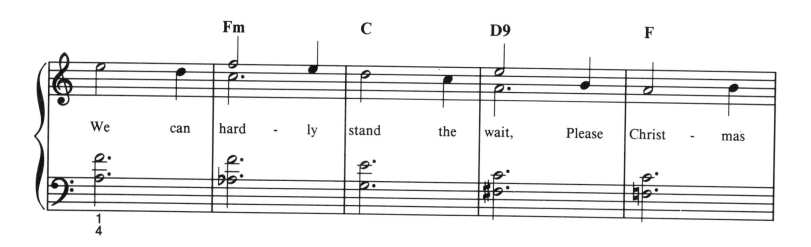

C-H-R-I-S-T-M-A-S

Words by JENNY LOU CARSON
Music by EDDY ARNOLD

Moderately

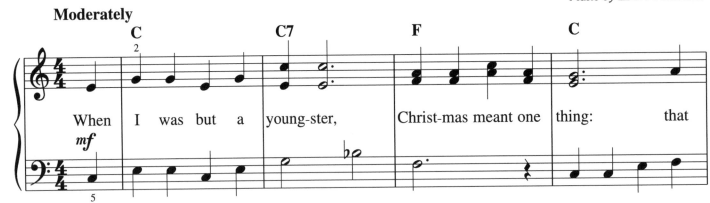

When I was but a young-ster, Christ-mas meant one thing: that

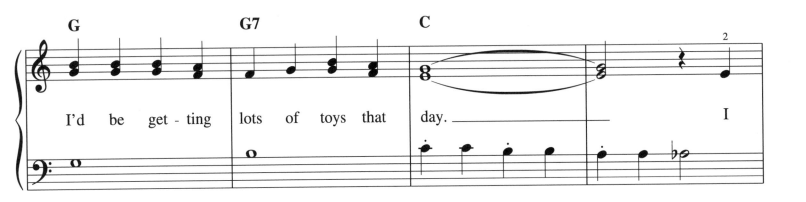

I'd be get-ting lots of toys that day. _____ I

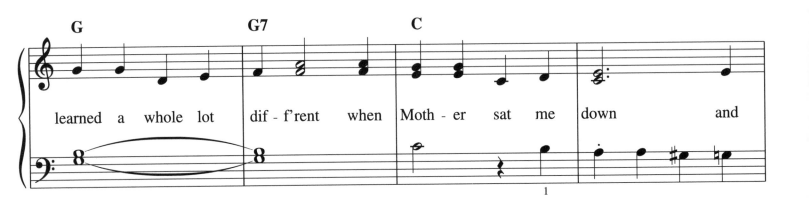

learned a whole lot dif-f'rent when Moth-er sat me down and

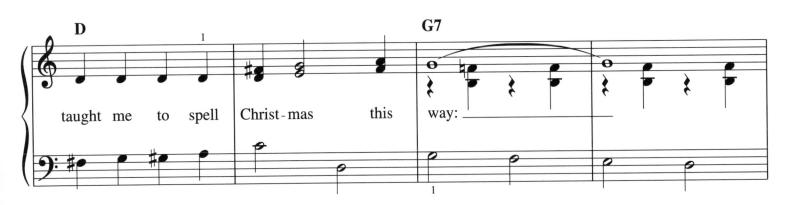

taught me to spell Christ-mas this way: _____

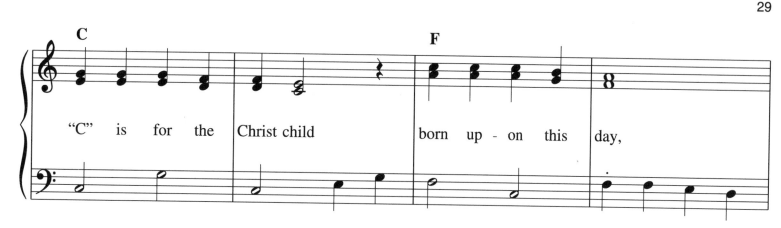

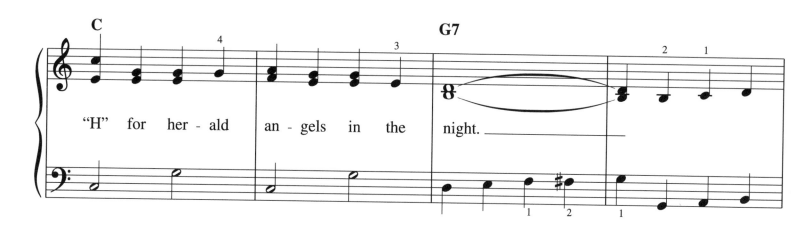

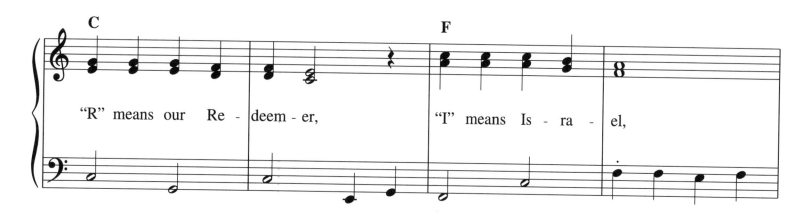

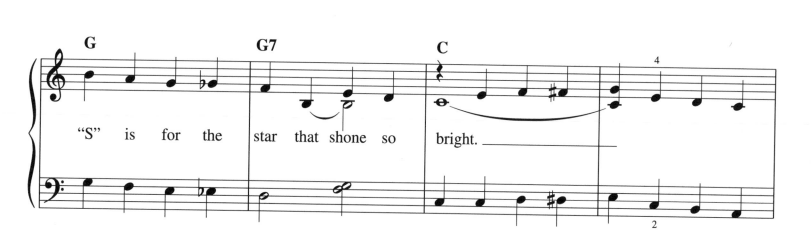

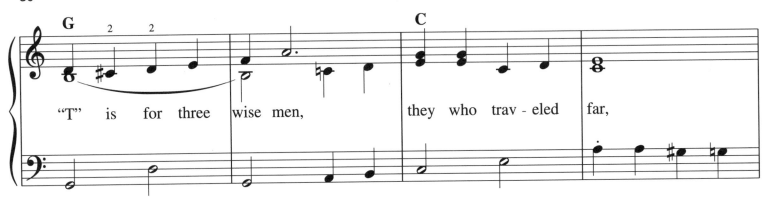

G

"T" is for three wise men,

C

they who trav - eled far,

D7

"M" is for the man - ger where He

G7

lay. _____

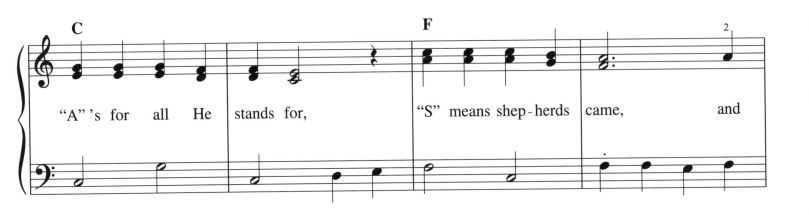

C

"A" 's for all He stands for,

F

"S" means shep - herds came, and

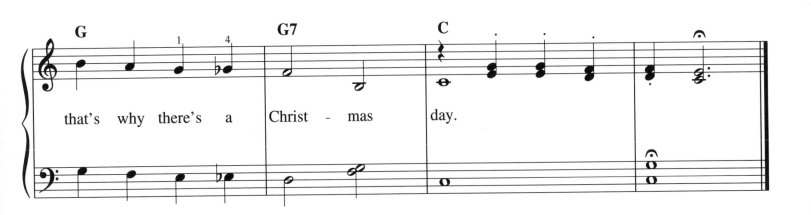

G

that's why there's a

G7

Christ - mas

C

day.

COVENTRY CAROL

Words by ROBERT CROO
Traditional English Melody

CHRISTMAS TIME IS HERE

Words by LEE MENDELSON
Music by VINCE GUARALDI

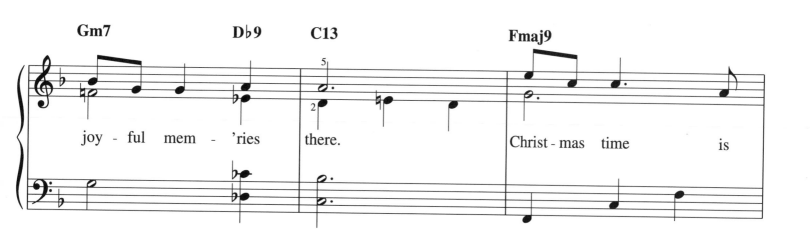

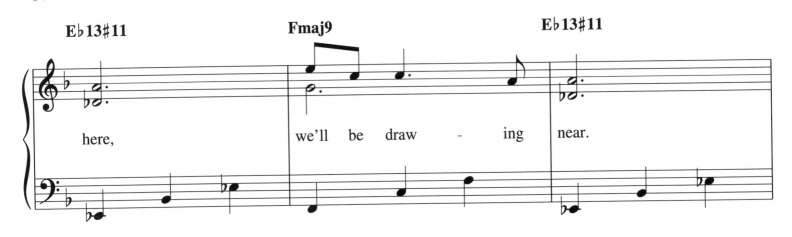

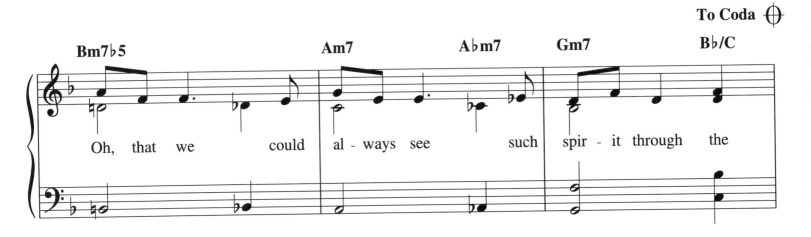

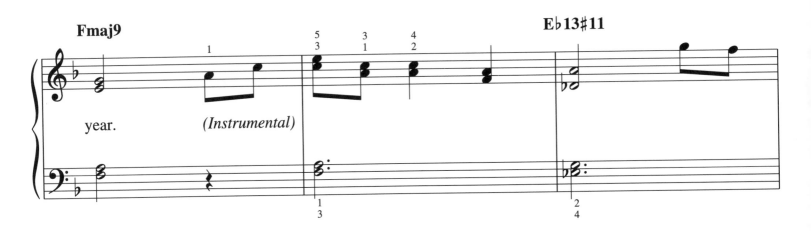

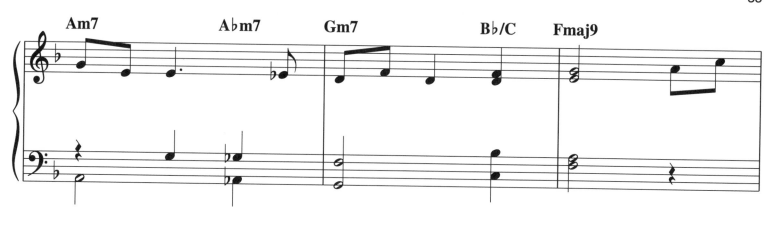

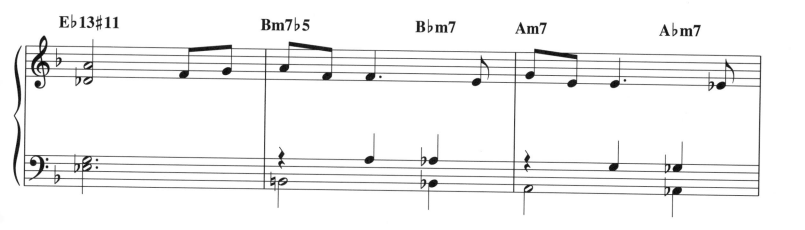

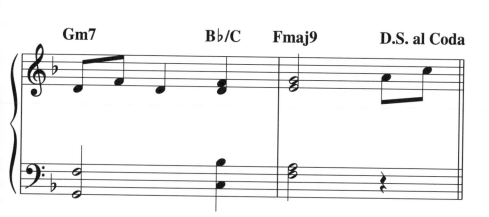

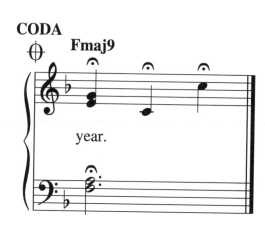

THE CHRISTMAS WALTZ

Words by SAMMY CAHN
Music by JULE STYNE

Moderately slow, with expression

Frost - ed win - dow panes, ___ can - dles gleam - ing in-

side, Paint - ed can - dy canes ___ on the tree; San - ta's

on his way, he's filled his sleigh with things, ___

___ things for you and for me. It's that time of year ___ when the

DANCE OF THE SUGAR PLUM FAIRY
from THE NUTCRACKER

By PYOTR IL'YICH TCHAIKOVSKY

Not too slow, daintily

GESU BAMBINO

Text by FREDERICK H. MARTENS
Music by PIETRO YON

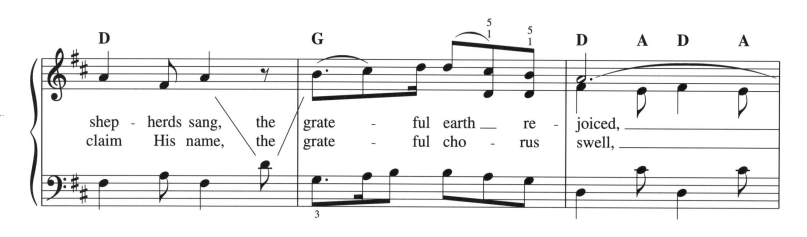

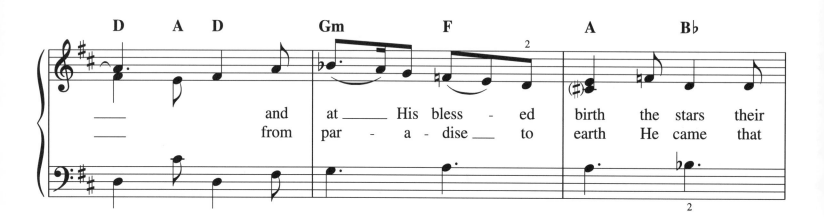

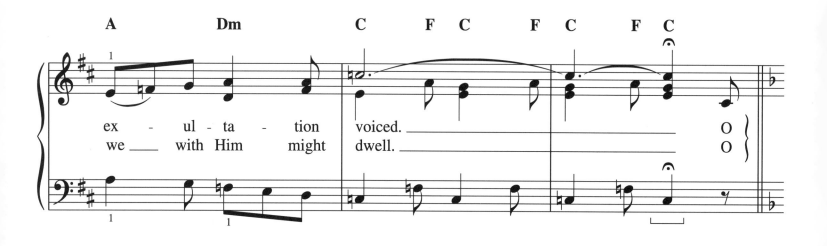

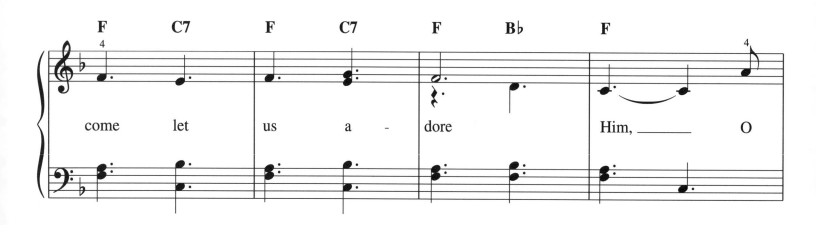

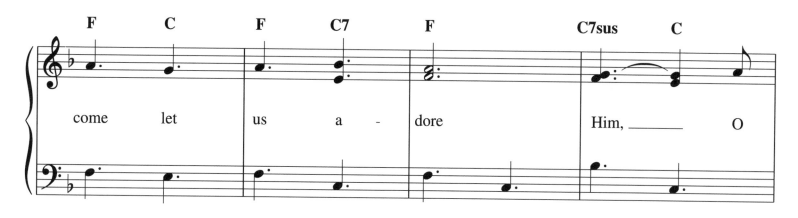

come let us a - dore Him, _____ O

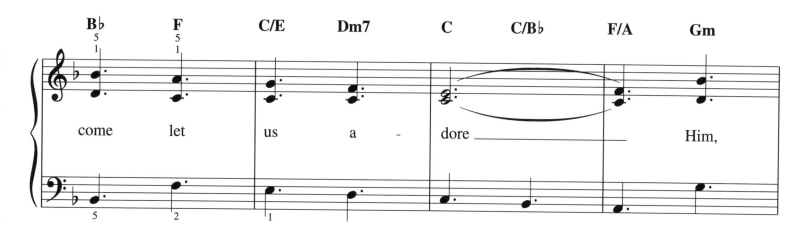

come let us a - dore _____ Him,

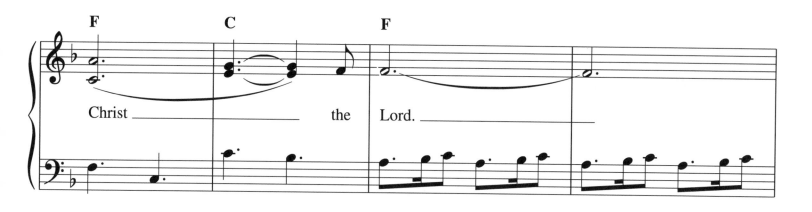

Christ _____ the Lord. _____

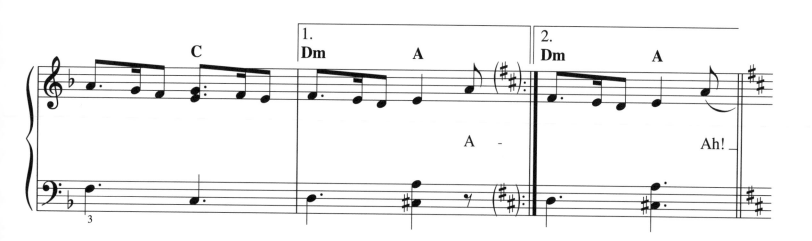

A - Ah! _____

42

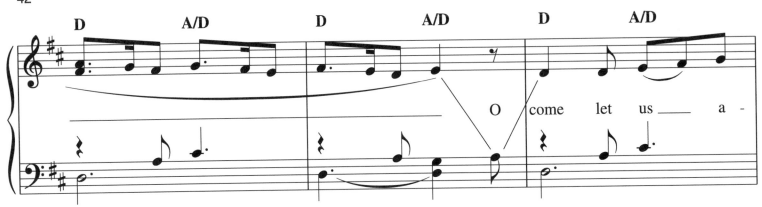

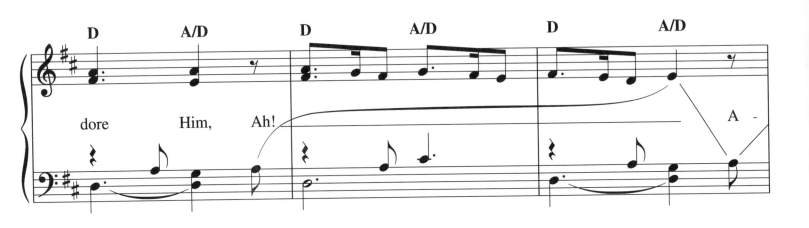

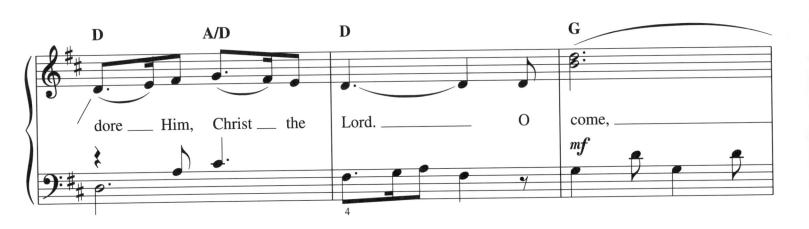

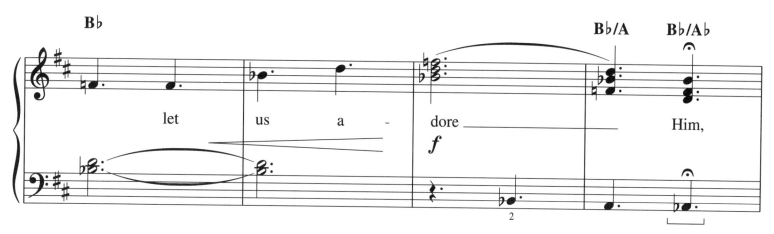

Italian Lyrics:

Nel l'umile capanna Nel freddo e povertá,
E nato il santo pargolo Che il mondo adorerá.
O-sanna, o-sanna cantano Con giubilante cor,
I tuoi pastori ed angeli O Re di lu-ce e amor

Venite adoriamo, Venite adoriamo, Venite adoriamo,
Gesu Redentor.

Oh bel bambin' non piangere, Non pianger Redentor,
La mamma tua cullandoti Ti bacia, O Salvator.
O-sanna, o-sanna cantano Con guibilante cor,
I tuoi pastori ed angeli O Re di luce e amore.

DECK THE HALL

Traditional Welsh Carol

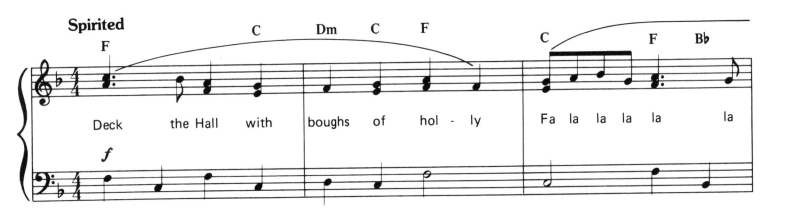

Deck the Hall with boughs of hol-ly Fa la la la la la

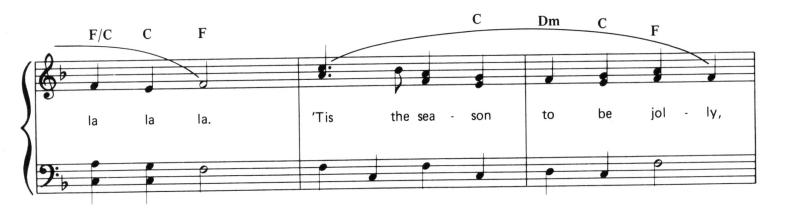

la la la. 'Tis the sea-son to be jol-ly,

Fa la la la la la la la la. Don we now our

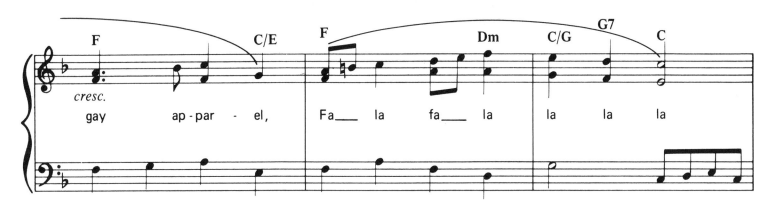

gay ap-par - el, Fa___ la fa___ la la la la

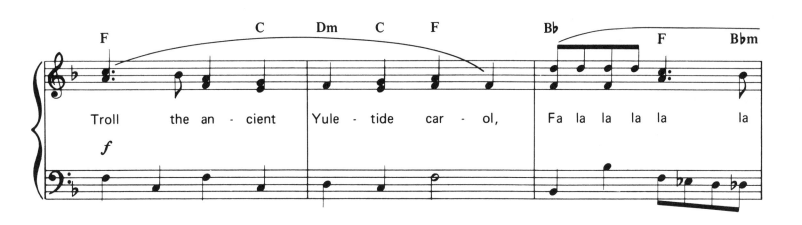

Troll the an - cient Yule - tide car - ol, Fa la la la la la

la la la. Fa la la la la la la

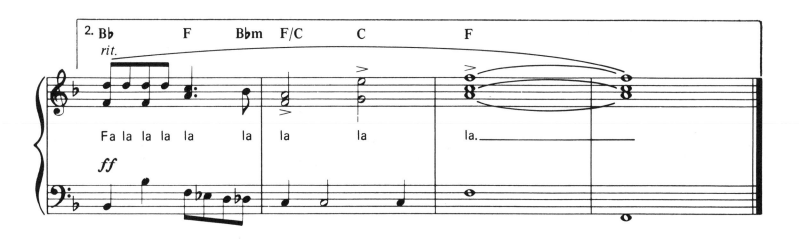

Fa la la la la la la la la.___

DO YOU HEAR WHAT I HEAR

Words and Music by NOEL REGNEY
and GLORIA SHAYNE

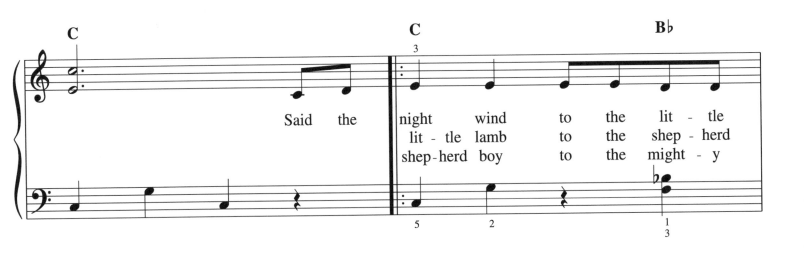

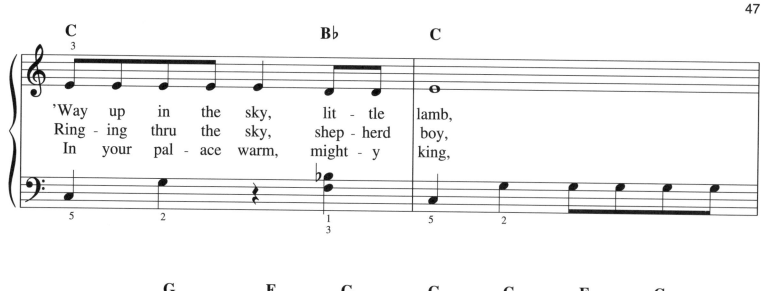

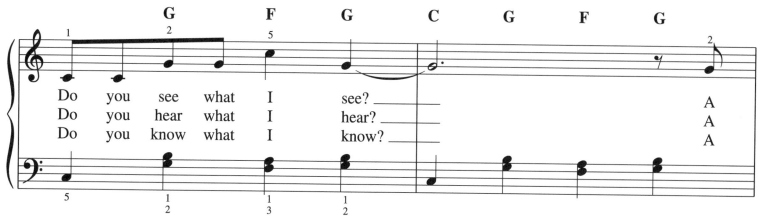

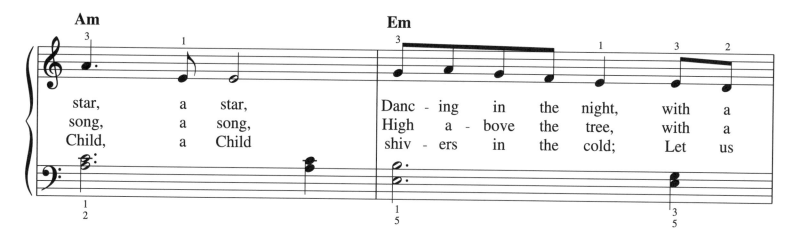

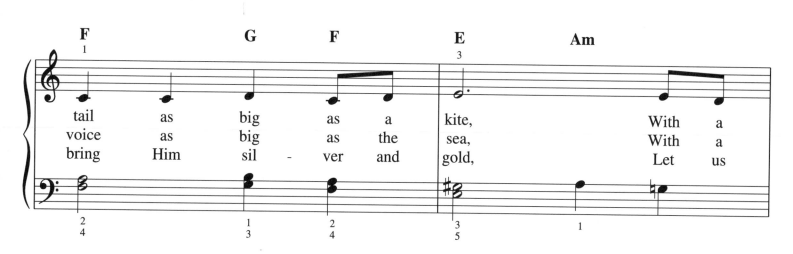

49

Child,   The Child,   sleep - ing   in   the   night,   He   will

bring   us   good - ness   and   light,   He   will

bring   us   good - ness   and   light.

50

THE FIRST NOEL

17th Century English Carol
Music from *W. Sandys' Christmas Carols*

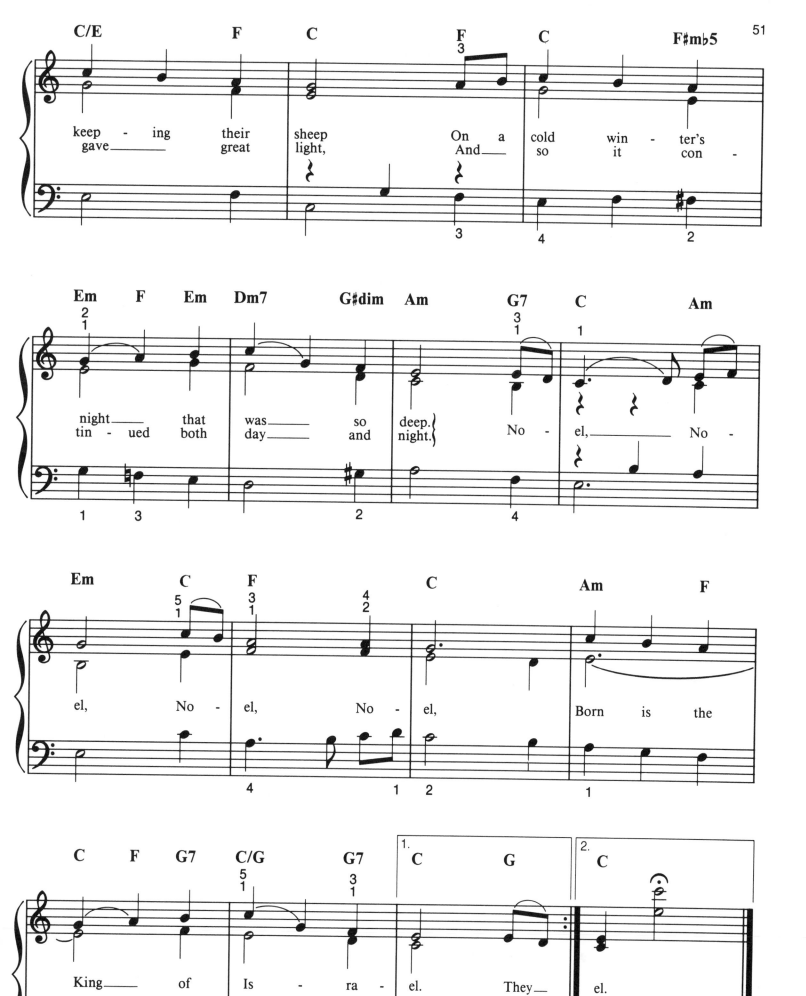

THE FRIENDLY BEASTS

Traditional English Carol

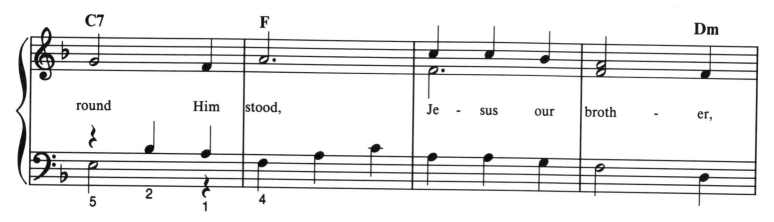

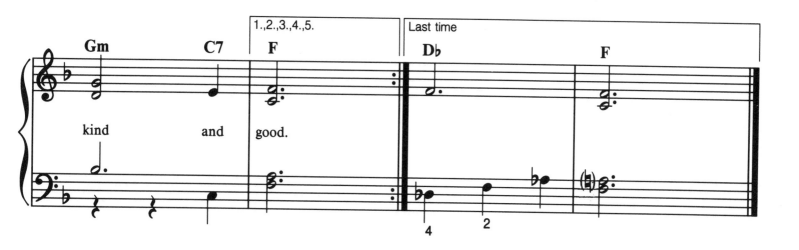

Additional Lyrics

2. "I," said the donkey, shaggy and brown,
   "I carried His mother up hill and down;
   I carried her safely to Bethlehem town."
   "I," said the donkey, shaggy and brown.

3. "I," said the cow all white and red,
   "I gave Him my manger for His bed;
   I gave Him my hay to pillow his head."
   "I," said the cow all white and red.

4. "I," said the sheep with curly horn,
   "I gave Him my wool for His blanket warm;
   He wore my coat on Christmas morn."
   "I," said the sheep with curly horn.

5. "I," said the dove from the rafters high,
   "I cooed Him to sleep so He would not cry,
   We cooed Him to sleep, my mate and I."
   "I," said the dove from the rafter high.

6. Thus every beast by some good spell,
   In the stable dark was glad to tell
   Of the gift he gave Emanuel,
   The gift he gave Emanuel.

FROSTY THE SNOW MAN

Words and Music by STEVE NELSON
and JACK ROLLINS

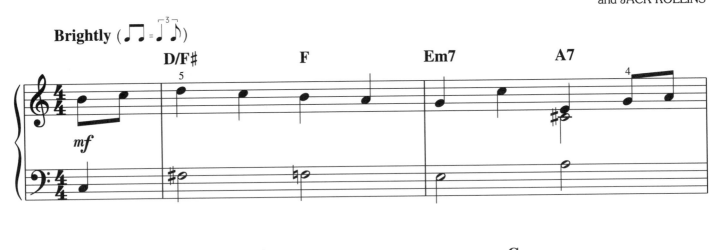

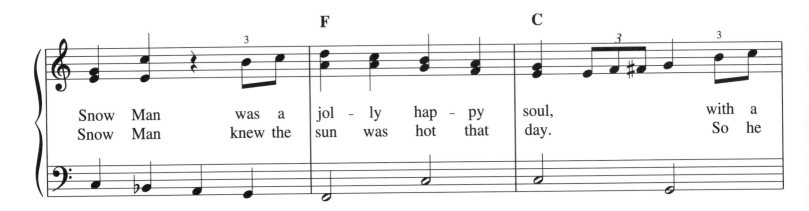

Frost - y the
Frost - y the

Snow Man   was a jol - ly hap - py soul,   with a
Snow Man   knew the sun was hot that day.   So he

corn - cob pipe and a but - ton nose and two eyes made out of
said, "Let's run and we'll have some fun now be - fore I melt a -

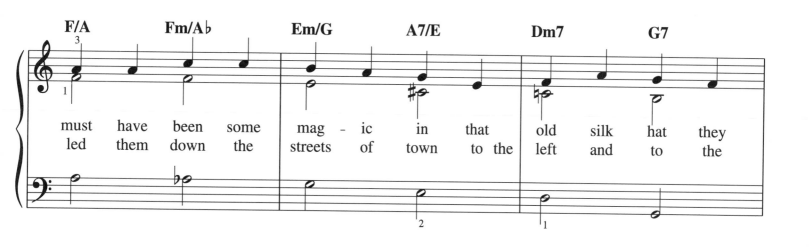

C   **G/D**

found,   for   when they placed it   on his head, he be -
right.   He   ran so fast he   dis - ap - peared, yep,

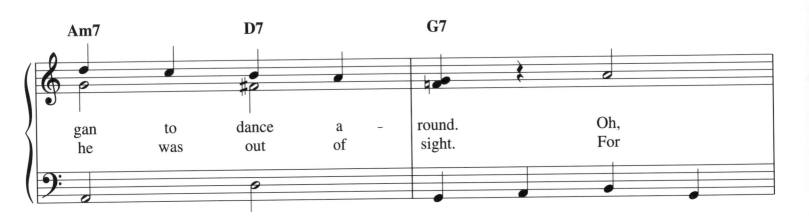

Am7   **D7**   **G7**

gan   to   dance   a - round.   Oh,
he   was   out   of   sight.   For

C   **C7**   **F**   **F♯dim7**

Frost - y   the   Snow Man   was a - live as he could
Frost - y   the   Snow Man   had to   hur - ry he on his

C/G   **A7**   **D/F♯**   **F**

be,   and the   chil - dren say   he could
way,   but he   waved good - bye,   say - in'

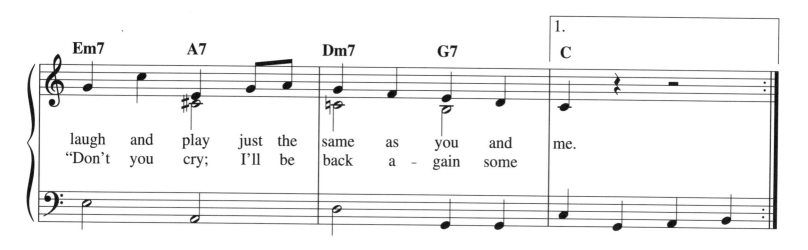

laugh and play just the same as you and me.
"Don't you cry; I'll be back a – gain some

day." Thump-e – ty thump thump thump-e – ty thump thump,

look at frost – y go! Thump-e – ty thump thump

thump-e – ty thump thump o – ver the hills of snow!

GO, TELL IT ON THE MOUNTAIN

African-American Spiritual
Verses by JOHN W. WORK, JR.

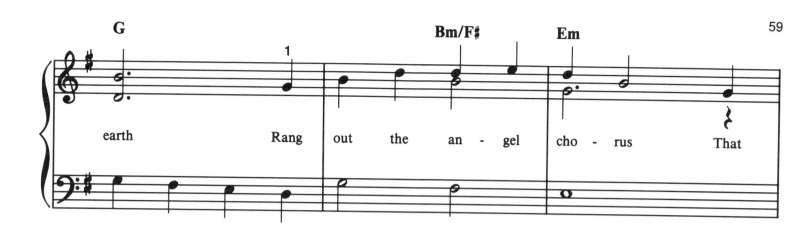

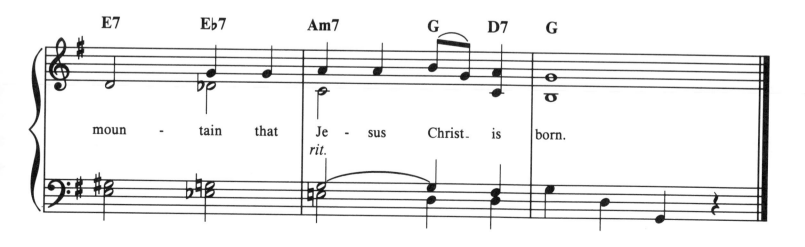

GOD REST YE MERRY, GENTLEMEN

19th Century English Carol

61

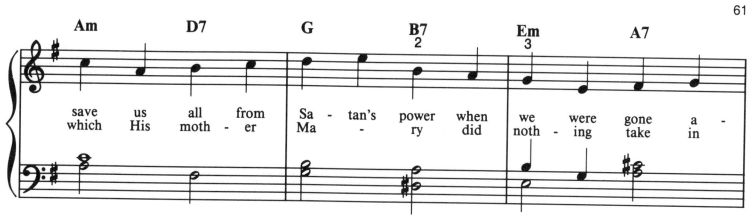

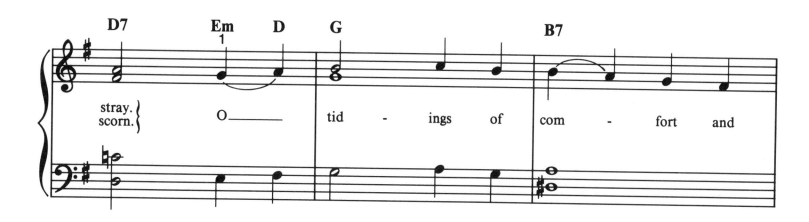

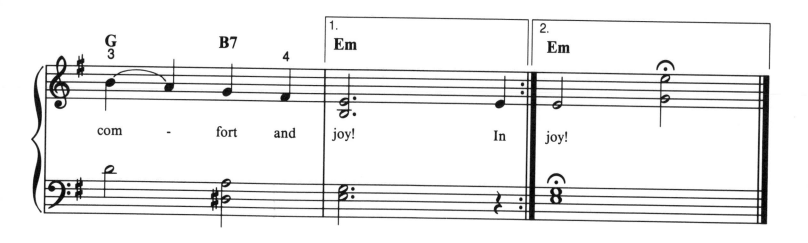

GOOD CHRISTIAN MEN, REJOICE

14th Century Latin Text
Translated by JOHN MASON NEALE
14th Century German Melody

Chris - tian men, re - joice with heart and soul and voice

Now ye hear of end - less bliss; Joy! Joy! Je - sus Christ was

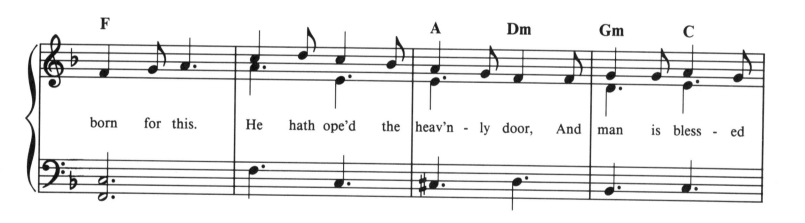

born for this. He hath ope'd the heav'n - ly door, And man is bless - ed

ev - er - more. Christ was born for this! Christ was born for this!

GOOD KING WENCESLAS

Words by JOHN M. NEALE
Music from *Piae Cantiones*

THE GREATEST GIFT OF ALL

Words and Music by
JOHN JARVIS

Moderately slow

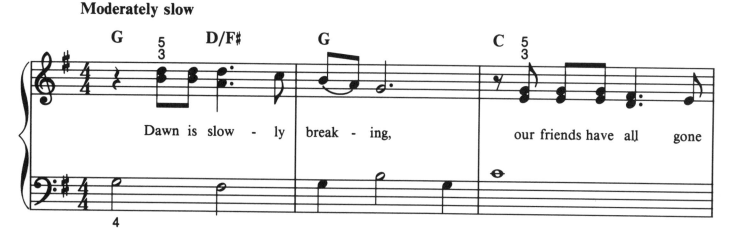

Dawn is slow - ly break - ing, our friends have all gone

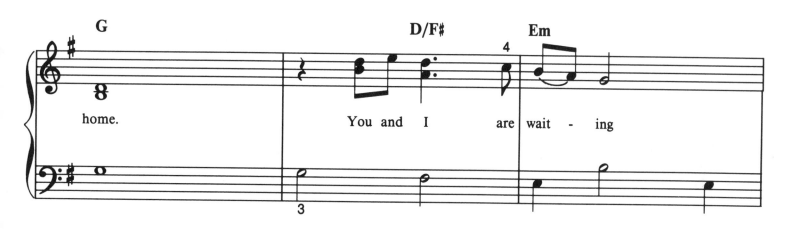

home. You and I are wait - ing

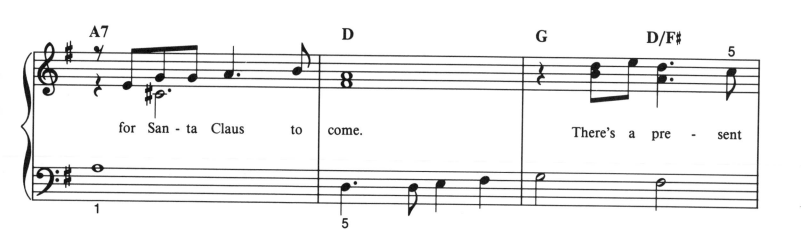

for San - ta Claus to come. There's a pre - sent

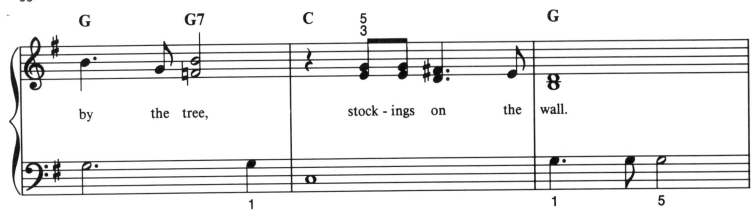

by the tree, stock-ings on the wall.

Know- ing you're in love with me is the great - est gift of ___

all. The fire is slow - ly

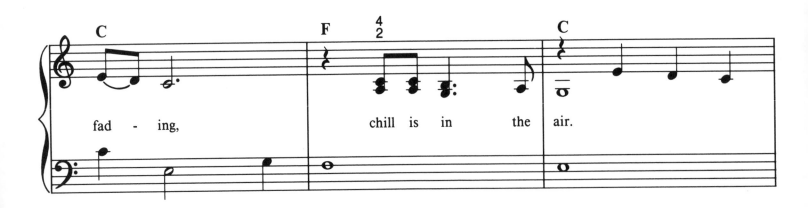

fad - ing, chill is in the air.

67

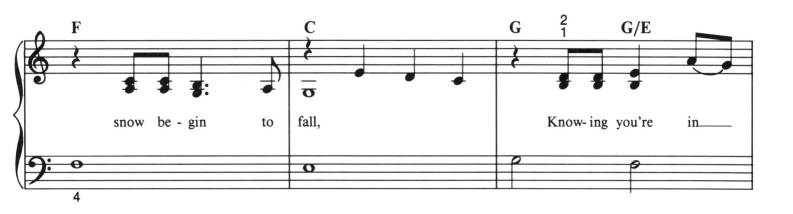

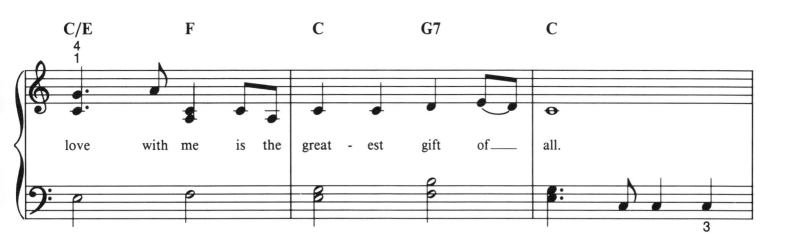

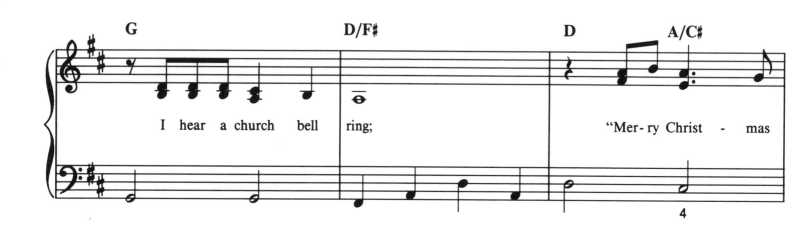

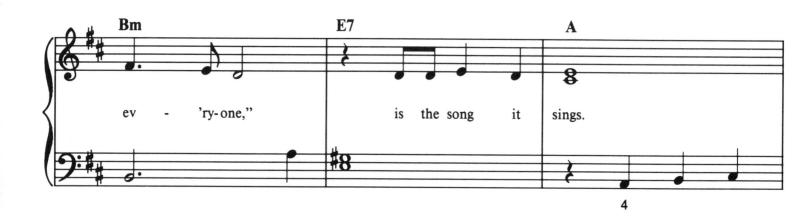

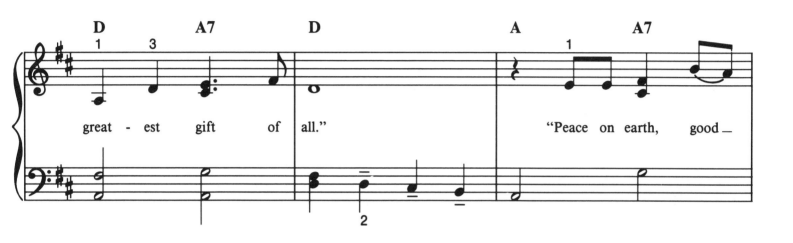

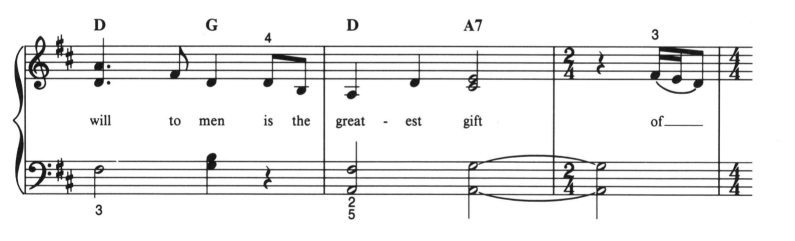

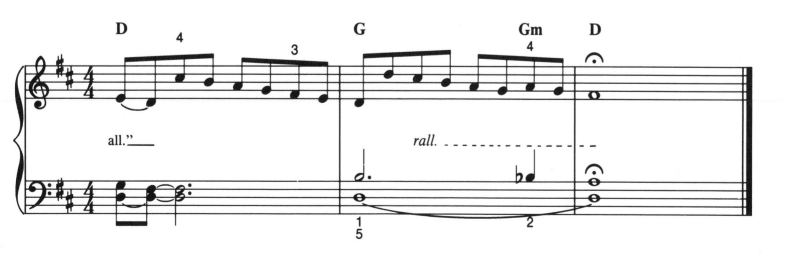

HAPPY HOLIDAY

from the Motion Picture Irving Berlin's HOLIDAY INN

Words and Music by
IRVING BERLIN

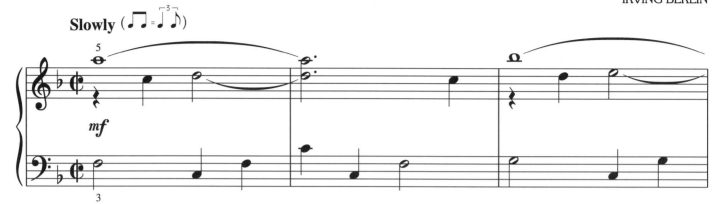

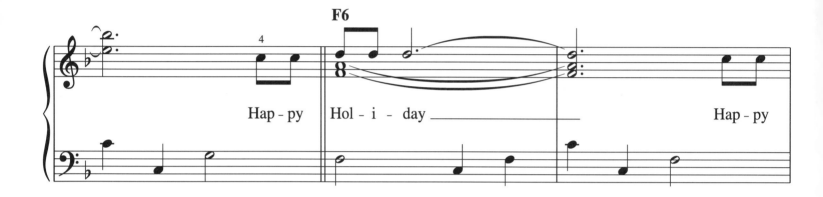

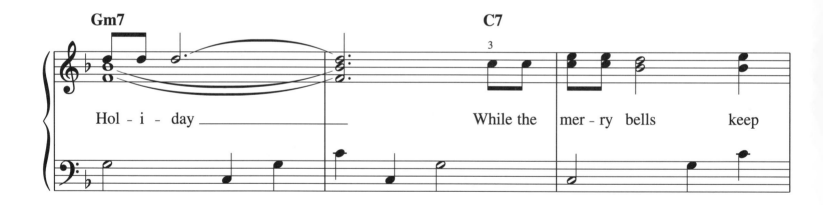

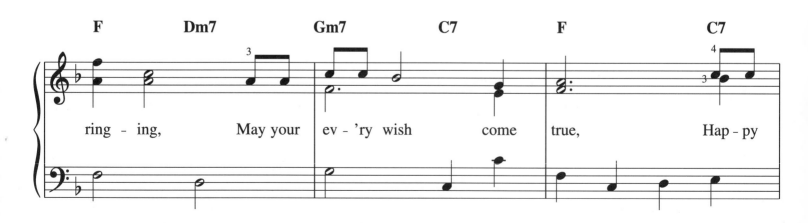

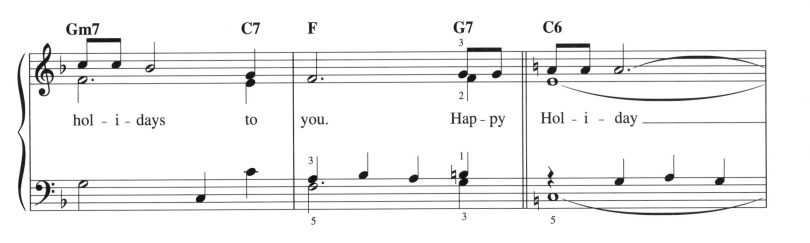

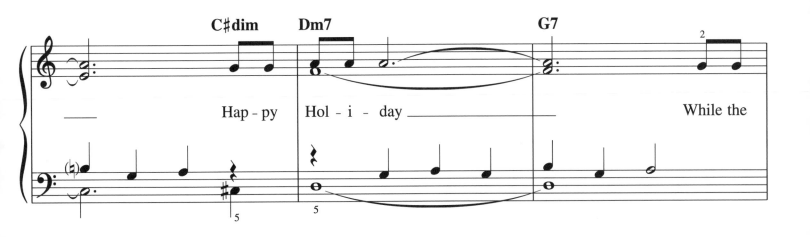

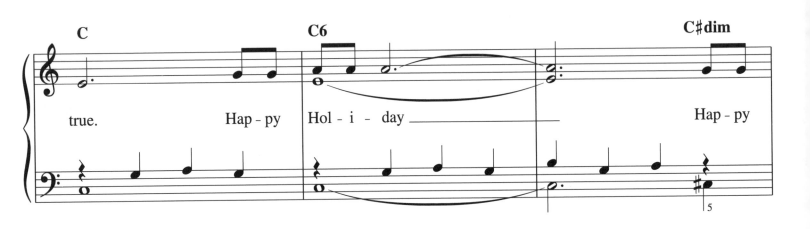

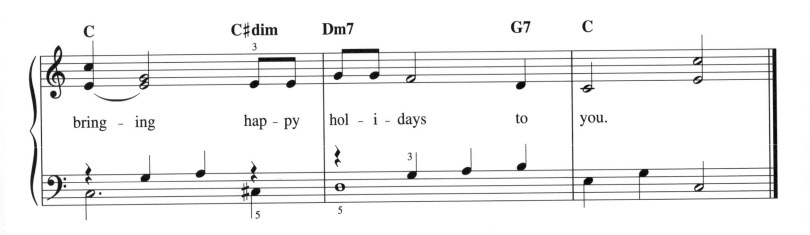

A HOLLY JOLLY CHRISTMAS

Music and Lyrics by
JOHNNY MARKS

Moderately

mf

Have a

C   C#dim

hol - ly jol - ly Christ - mas, it's the best time of the

G7   Gdim   G7

year. I don't know if there'll be snow but have a cup of

C

cheer. Have a hol - ly jol - ly Christ - mas, and when

74

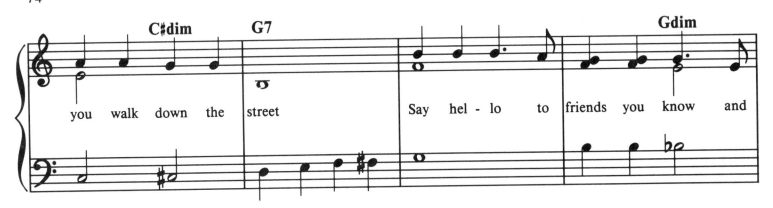

you walk down the street   Say hel - lo to friends you know and

ev - 'ry - one you meet.   Oh, ho, the

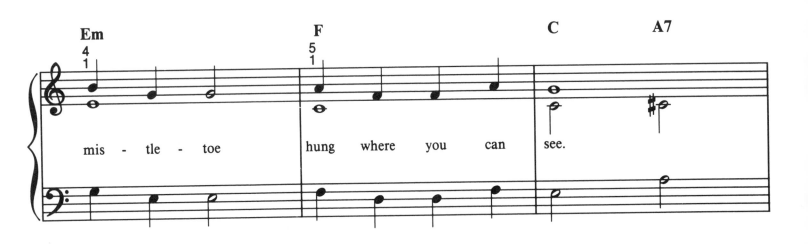

mis - tle - toe   hung where you can   see.

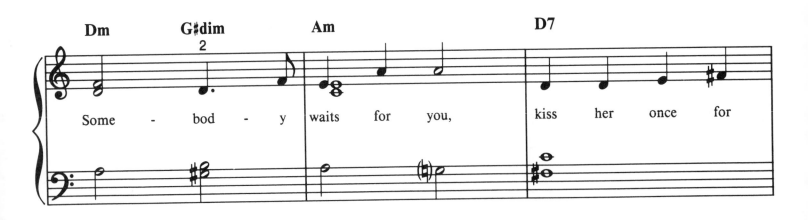

Some - bod - y waits for you,   kiss her once for

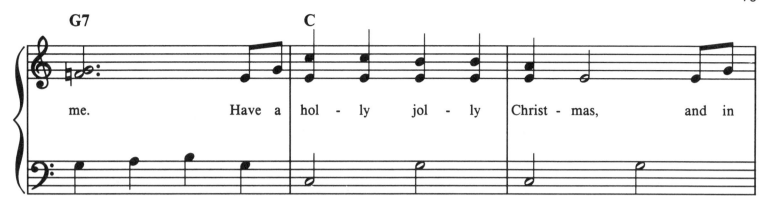

me. Have a hol - ly jol - ly Christ - mas, and in

case you did - n't hear Oh, by gol - ly, have a

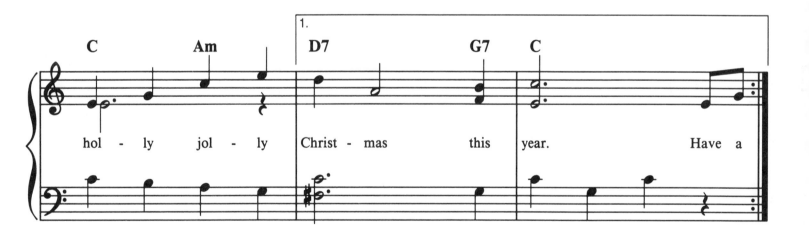

hol - ly jol - ly Christ - mas this year. Have a

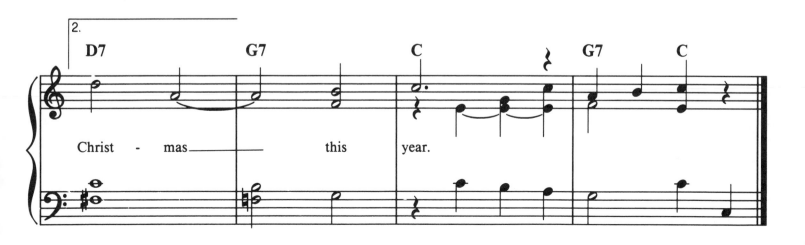

Christ - mas this year.

HAPPY XMAS
(War Is Over)

Words and Music by JOHN LENNON
and YOKO ONO

Moderately

So this is X - mas
X - mas

and what have you done,
and what have we done,

an-oth-er year o-ver,
an-oth-er year o-ver,

a new one just be- gun. _____
a new one just be- gun. _____

And so this is X-mas,
And so hap-py X-mas,

HARK! THE HERALD ANGELS SING

Words by CHARLES WESLEY
Altered by GEORGE WHITEFIELD
Music by FELIX MENDELSSOHN-BARTHOLDY
Arranged by WILLIAM H. CUMMINGS

81

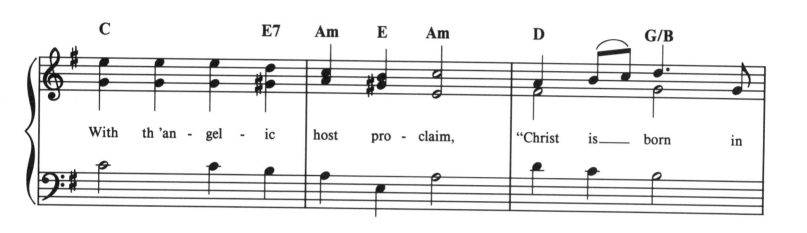

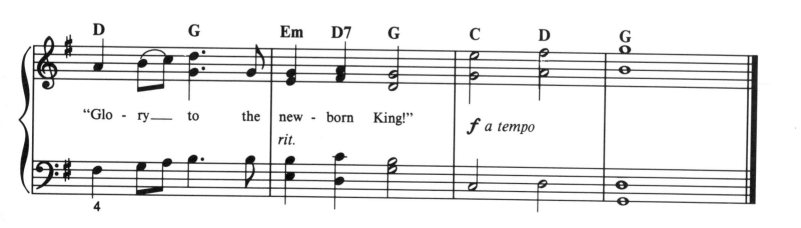

HERE WE COME A-WASSAILING

Traditional

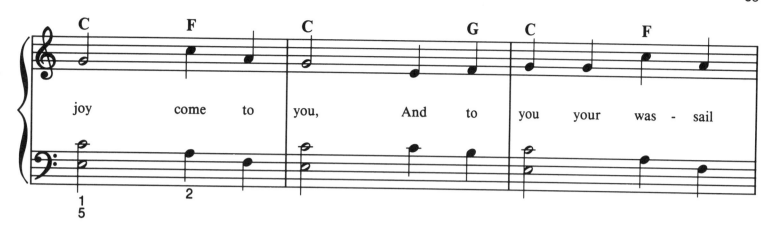

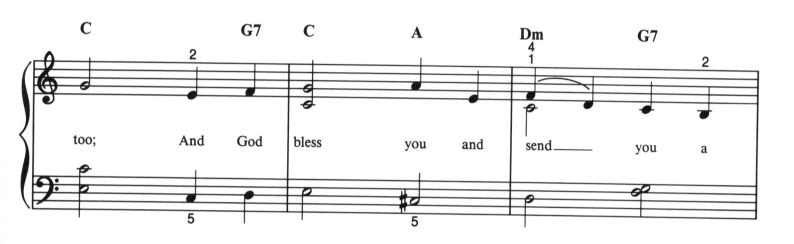

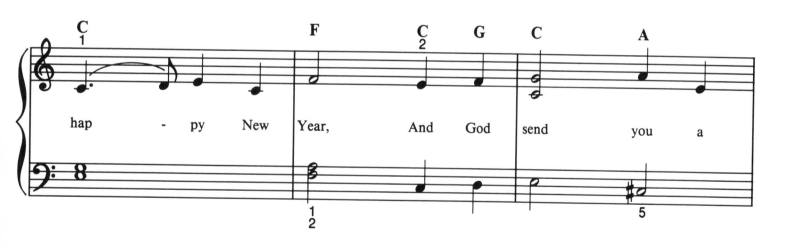

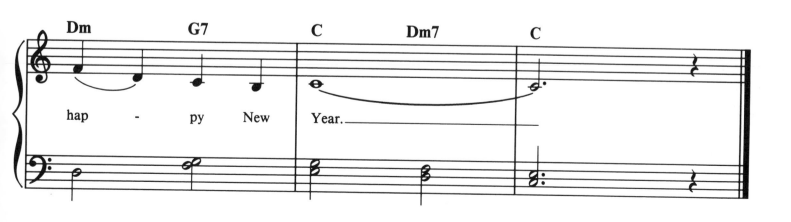

THE HOLLY AND THE IVY

18th Century English Carol

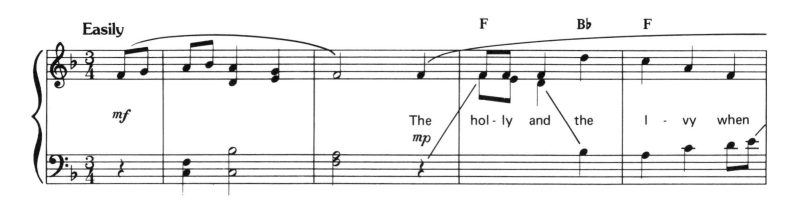

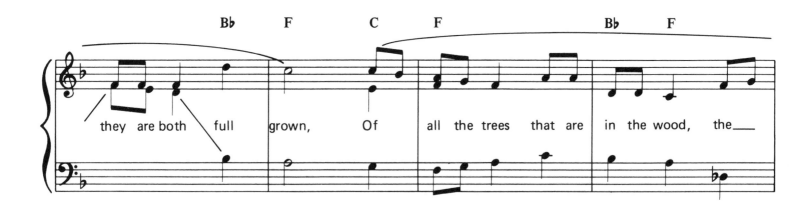

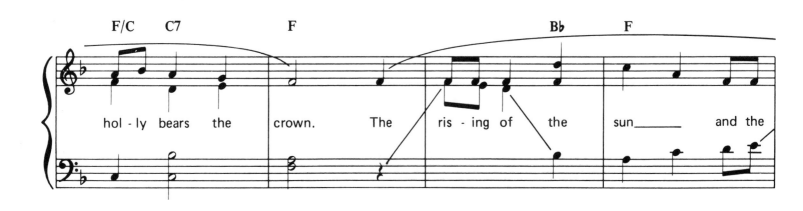

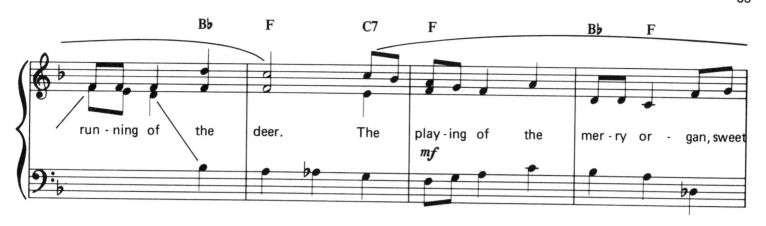

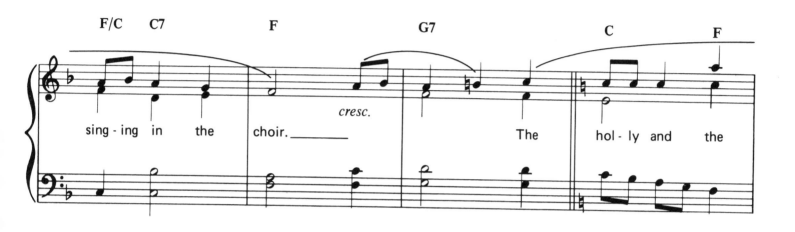

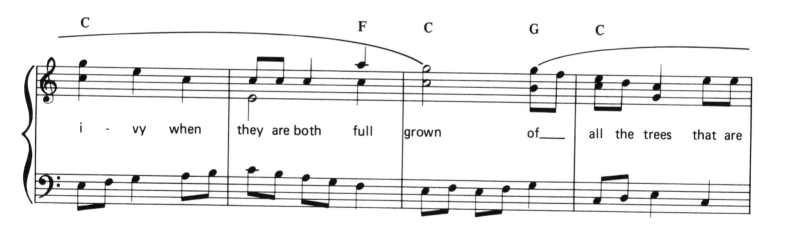

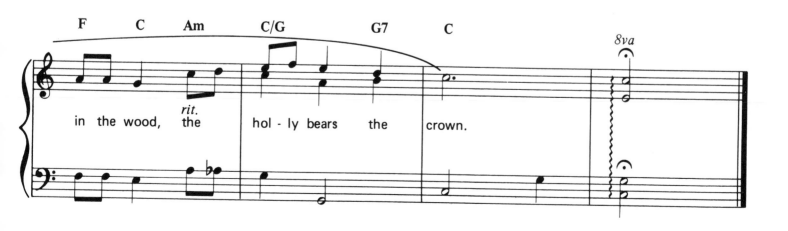

(There's No Place Like)
HOME FOR THE HOLIDAYS

Words by AL STILLMAN
Music by ROBERT ALLEN

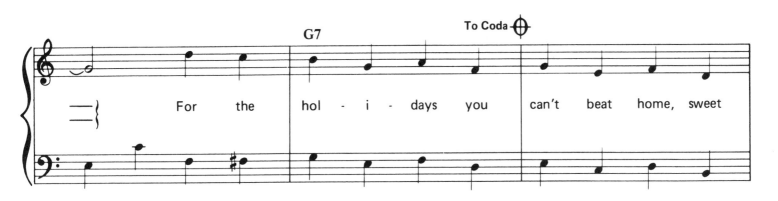

For the hol - i - days you can't beat home, sweet

home. I met a man who lives in

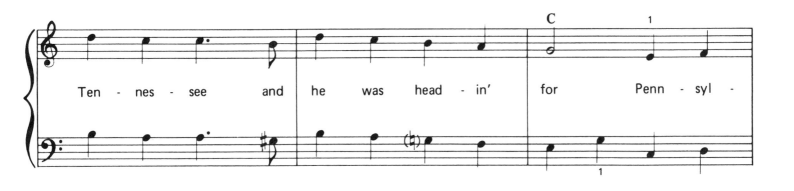

Ten - nes - see and he was head - in' for Penn - syl -

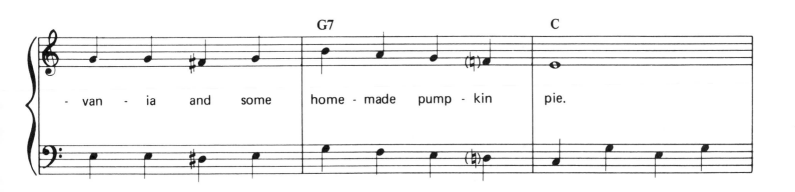

- van - ia and some home - made pump - kin pie.

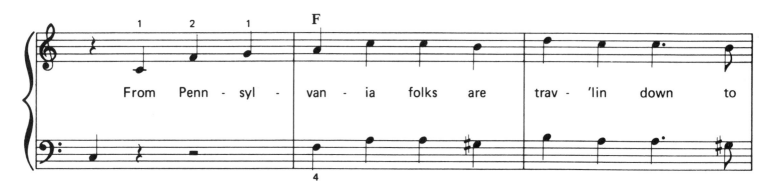

From Penn - syl - van - ia folks are trav - 'lin down to

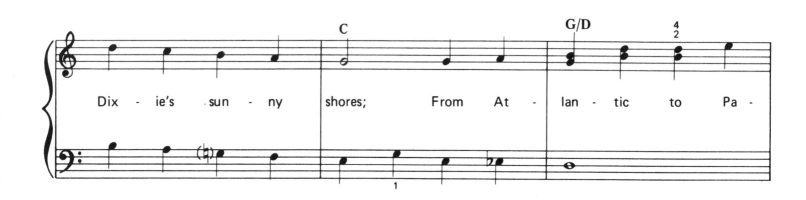

Dix - ie's sun - ny shores; From At - lan - tic to Pa -

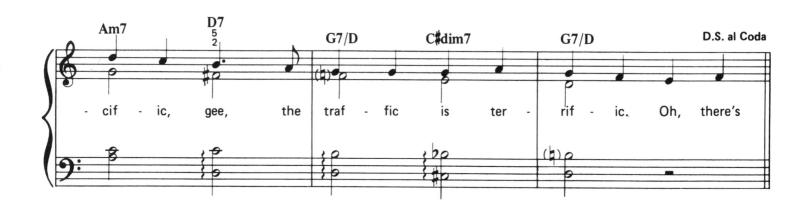

- cif - ic, gee, the traf - fic is ter - rif - ic. Oh, there's

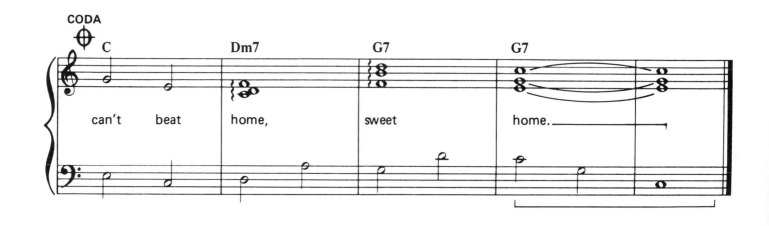

can't beat home, sweet home.

HYMNE

By VANGELIS

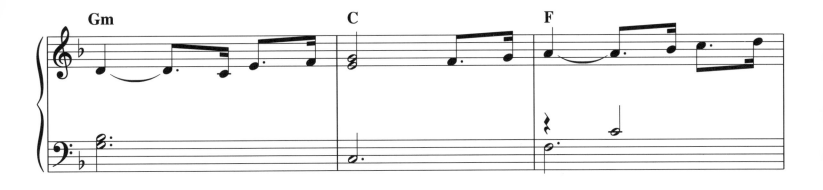

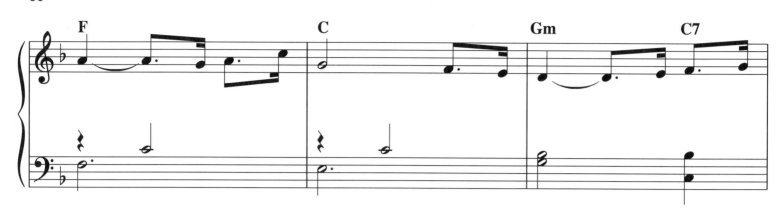

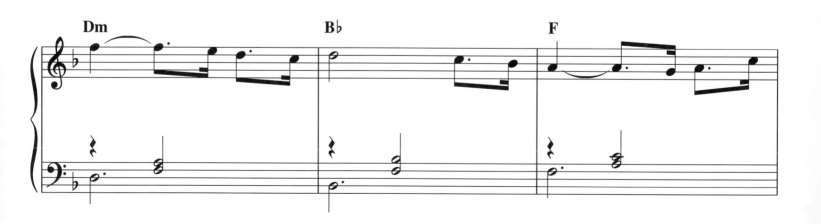

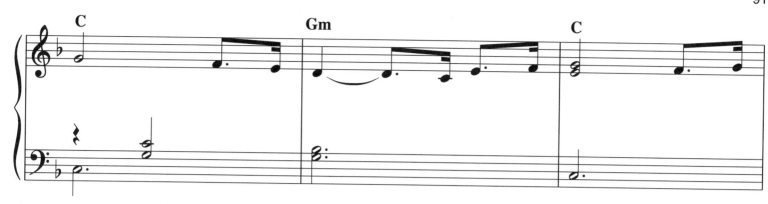

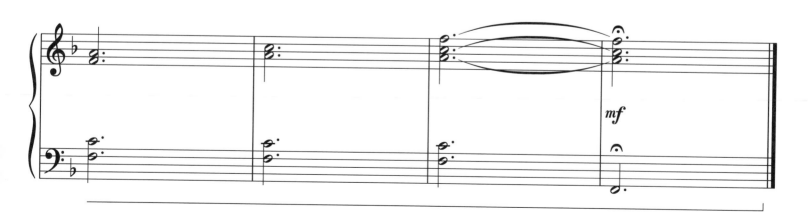

I HEARD THE BELLS
ON CHRISTMAS DAY

Words by HENRY WADSWORTH LONGFELLOW
Music by JOHN BAPTISTE CALKIN

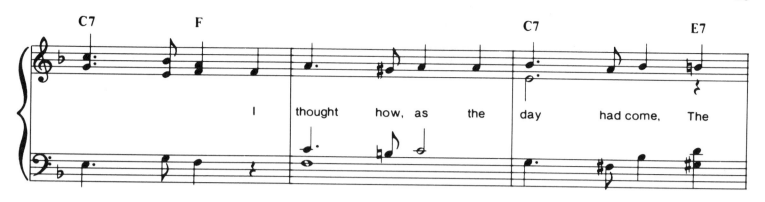

I thought how, as the day had come, The

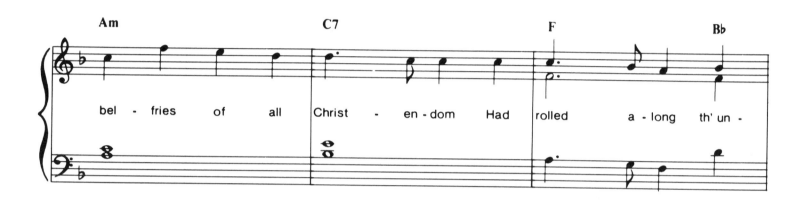

bel - fries of all Christ - en - dom Had rolled a - long th' un -

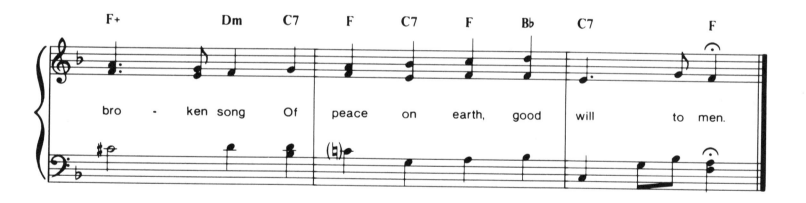

bro - ken song Of peace on earth, good will to men.

3. And in despair I bow'd my head:
"There is no peace on earth," I said,
"For hate is strong, and mocks the song
Of peace on earth, good will to men."

4. Then pealed the bells more loud and deep:
"God is not dead, nor doth He sleep;
The wrong shall fail, the right prevail,
With peace on earth, good will to men."

5. Till, ringing, singing on its way,
The world revolved from night to day,
A voice, a chime, a chant sublime,
Of peace on earth, good will to men!

I HEARD THE BELLS
ON CHRISTMAS DAY

Words by HENRY WADSWORTH LONGFELLOW
Adapted by JOHNNY MARKS
Music by JOHNNY MARKS

bel - fries of all Chris - ten - dom Had rung so long the un-

bro - ken song Of peace on earth good will to men.

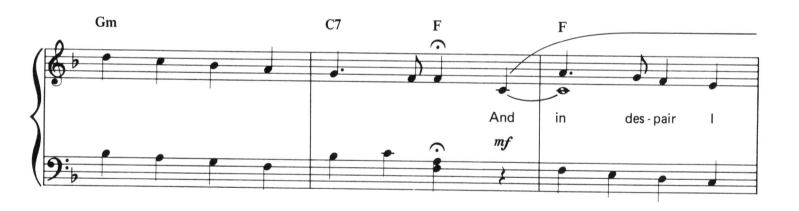

And in des - pair I

bowed my head. "There is no peace on earth," I said, "For

96

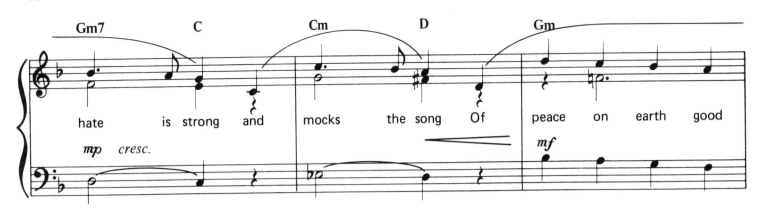

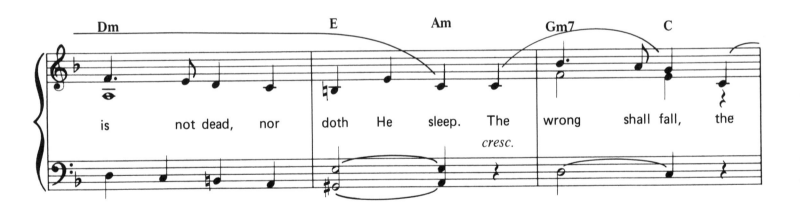

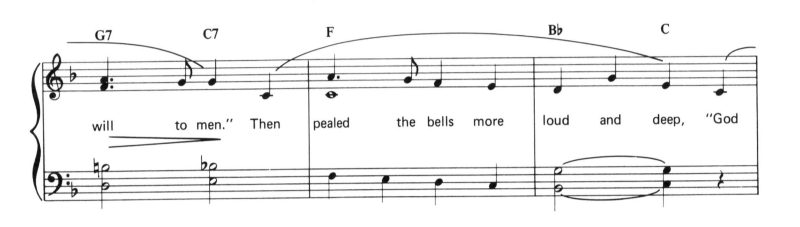

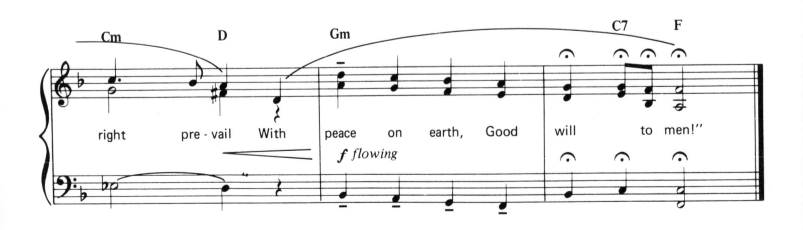

I SAW MOMMY KISSING SANTA CLAUS

Words and Music by
TOMMIE CONNOR

Moderately, with a lilt

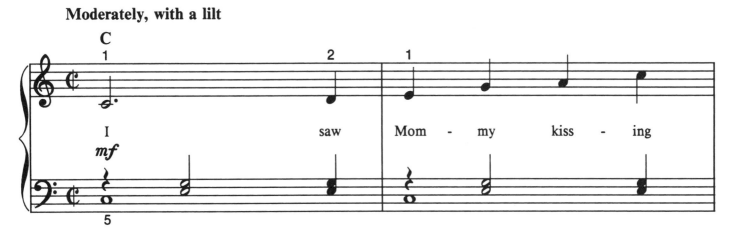

I saw Mom - my kiss - ing

San - ta Claus un - der - neath the

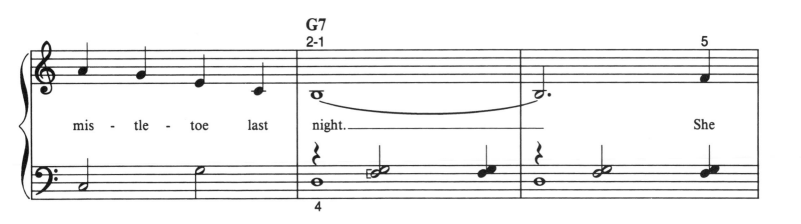

mis - tle - toe last night. She

98

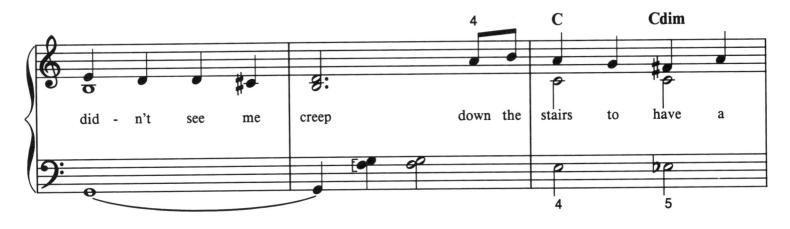

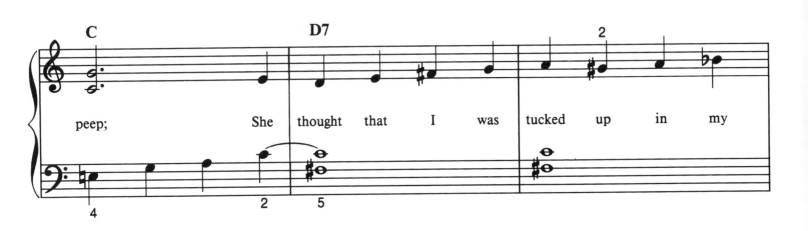

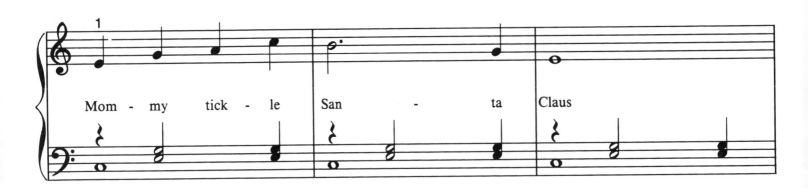

99

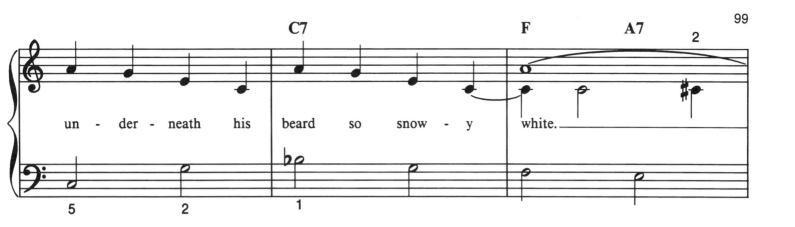

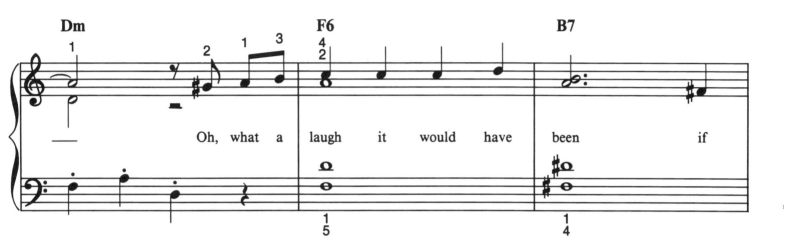

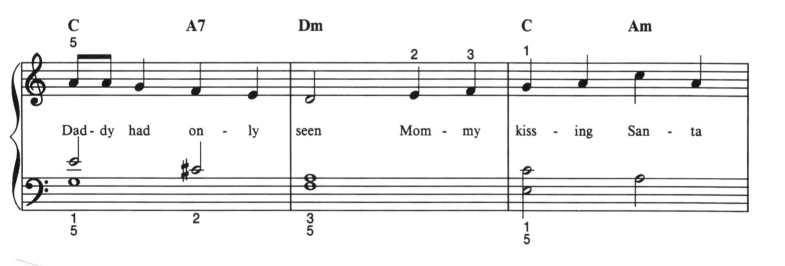

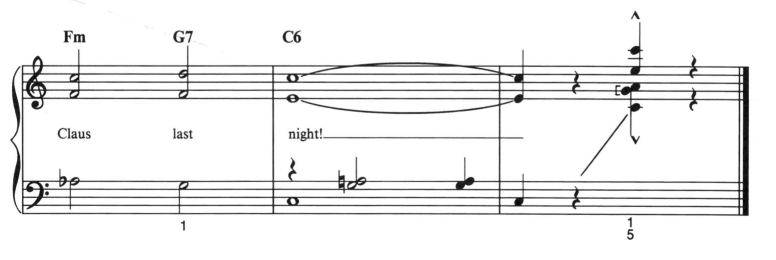

I SAW THREE SHIPS

Traditional English Carol

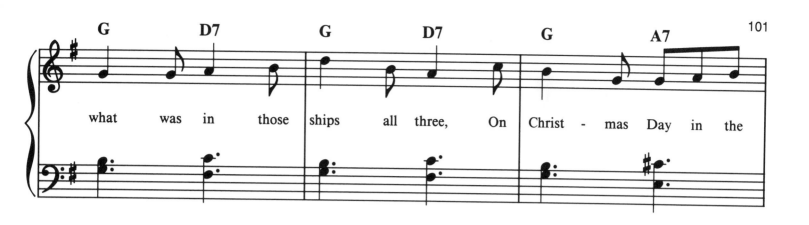

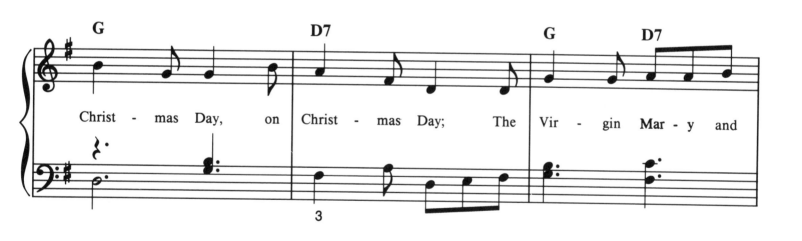
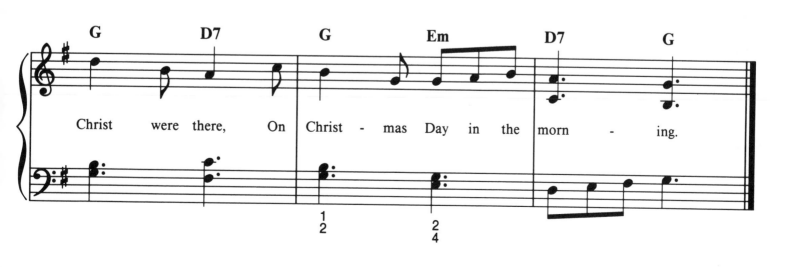

I'LL BE HOME FOR CHRISTMAS

Words and Music by KIM GANNON
and WALTER KENT

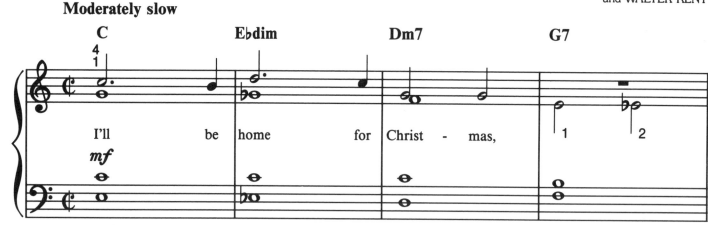

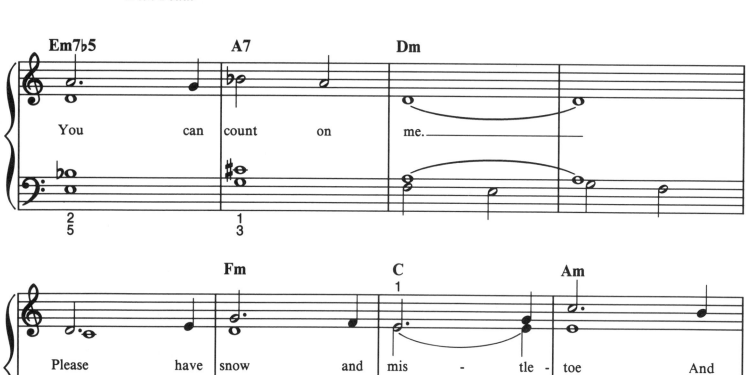

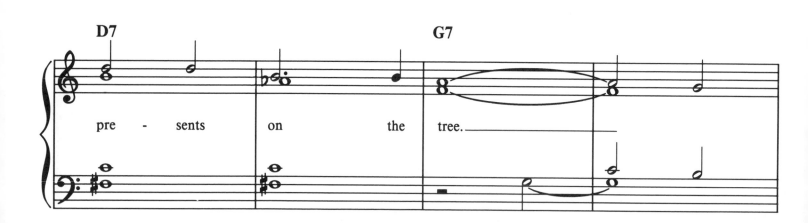

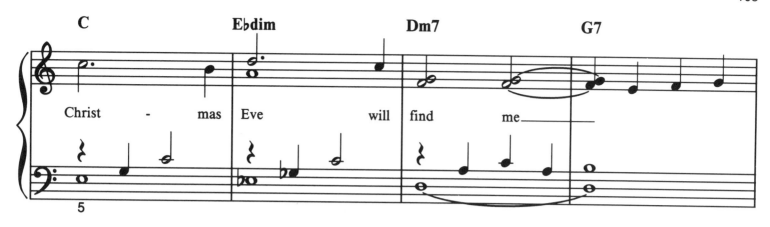

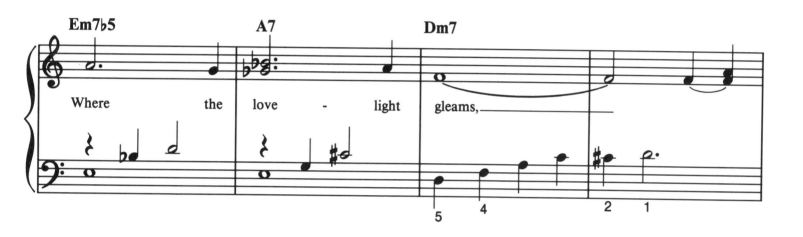

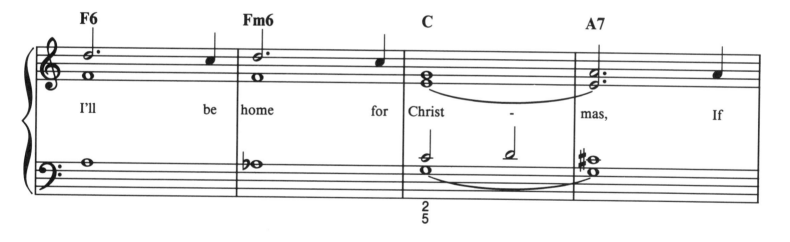

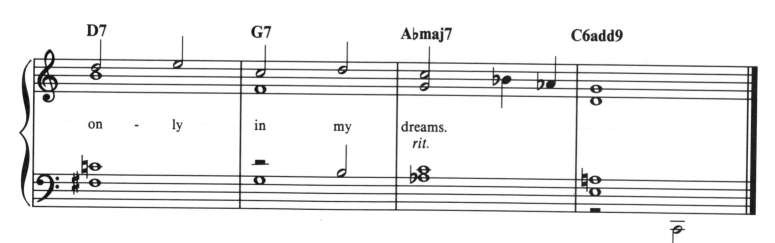

I'VE GOT MY LOVE
TO KEEP ME WARM

from the 20th Century Fox Motion Picture ON THE AVENUE

Words and Music by
IRVING BERLIN

Moderately

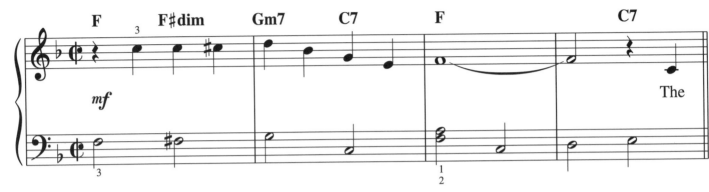

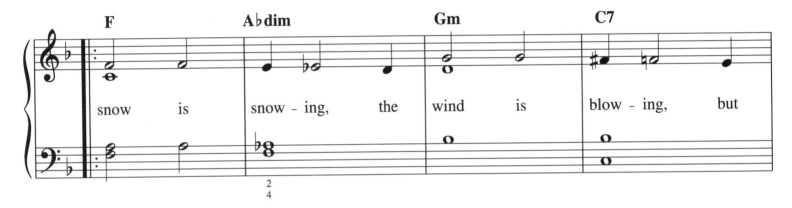

snow is snow - ing, the wind is blow - ing, but

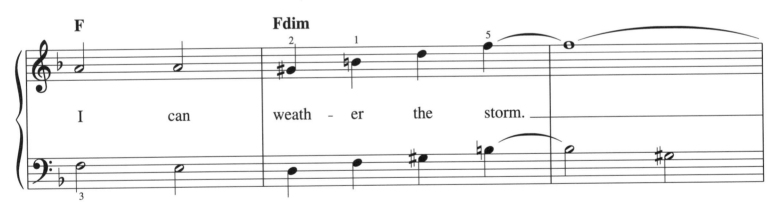

I can weath - er the storm.

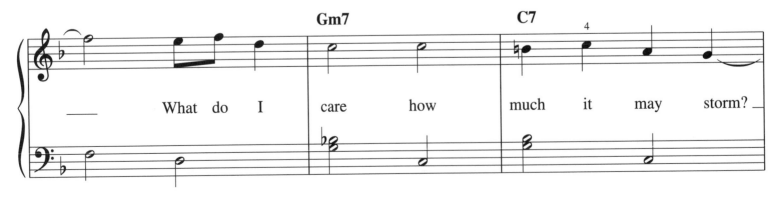

What do I care how much it may storm?

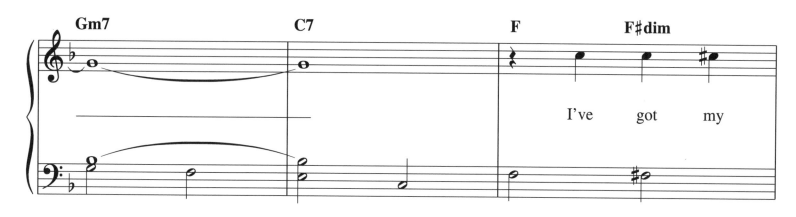

I've got my

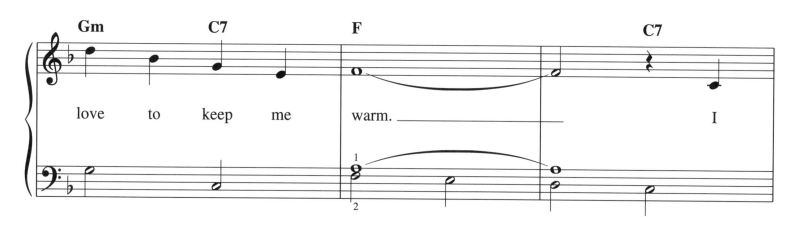

love to keep me warm. I

can't re — mem — ber a worse De —

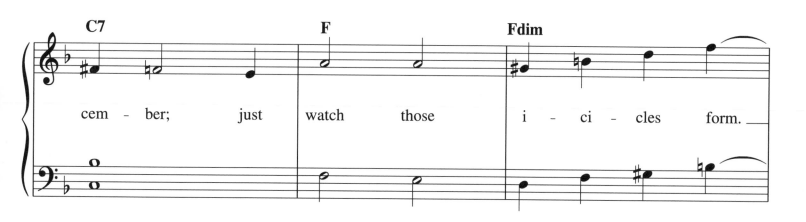

cem — ber; just watch those i — ci — cles form.

Gm7

What do I care if

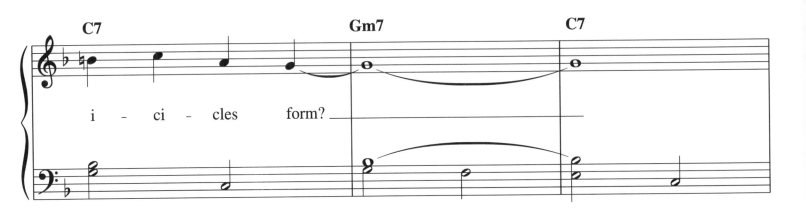

C7   **Gm7**   **C7**

i - ci - cles form? _____

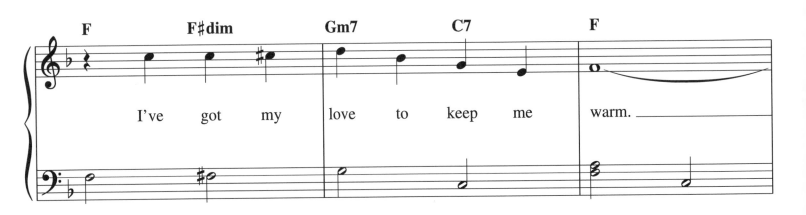

F   **F#dim**   **Gm7**   **C7**   **F**

I've got my love to keep me warm. _____

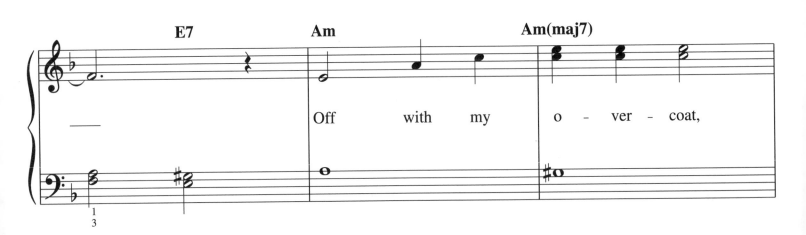

E7   **Am**   **Am(maj7)**

Off with my o - ver - coat,

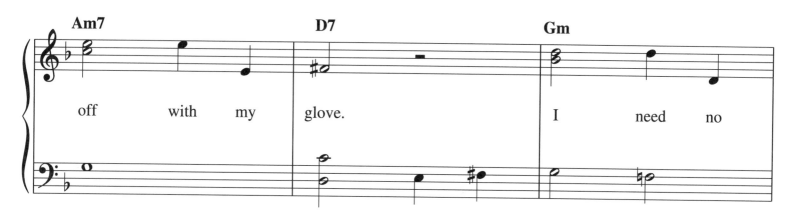

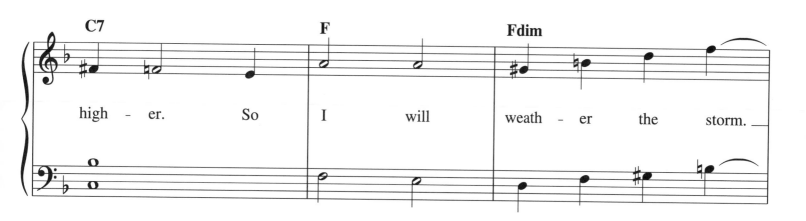

What do I care how

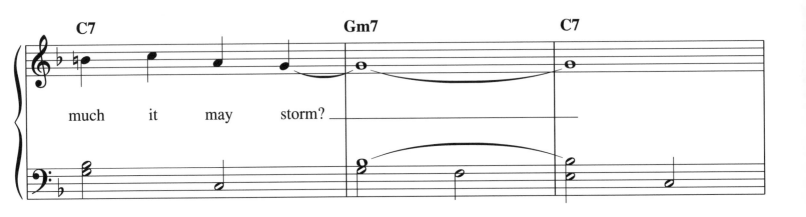

much it may storm?

I've got my love to keep me warm.

The warm.

JESU, JOY OF MAN'S DESIRING

By JOHANN SEBASTIAN BACH

Slowly and evenly

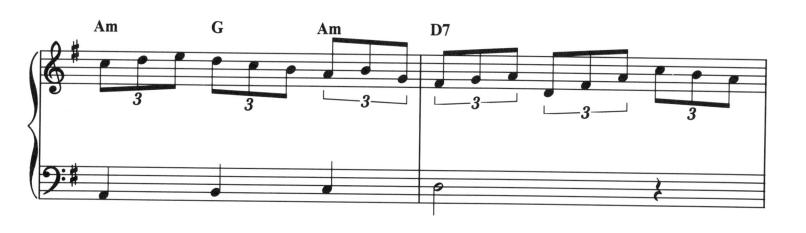

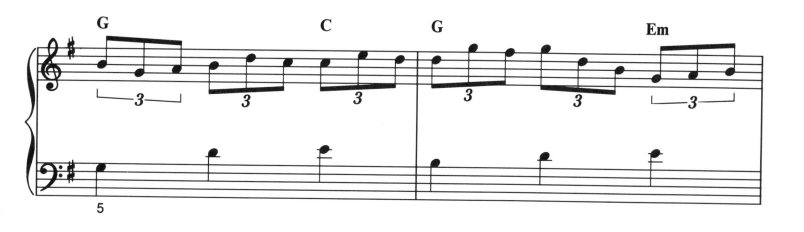

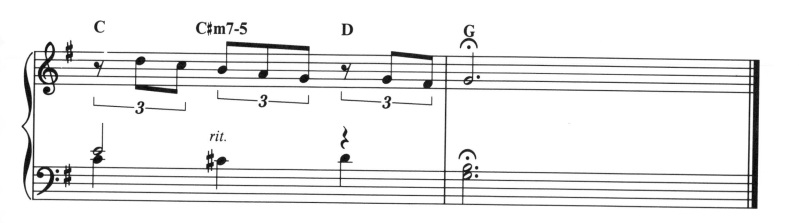

IT CAME UPON THE MIDNIGHT CLEAR

Words by EDMUND HAMILTON SEARS
Music by RICHARD STORRS WILLIS

113

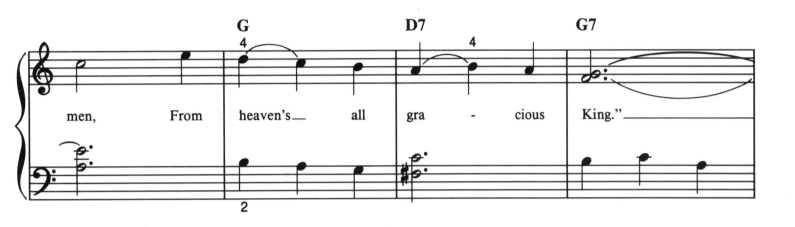

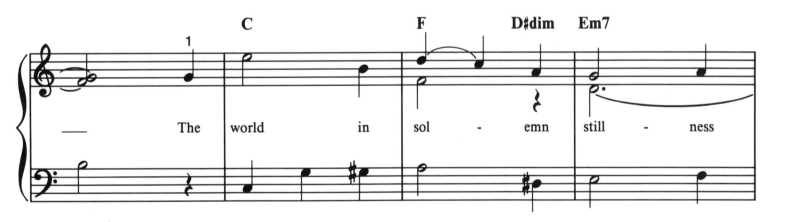

JESUS BORN ON THIS DAY

Words and Music by MARIAH CAREY
and WALTER AFANASIEFF

116

child is born on earth.) He is light, He is love, He is grace, born on Christ-mas

day. He is light, He is love, He is grace, born on Christ-mas

day. He is light, He is love, He is grace, born on Christ-mas

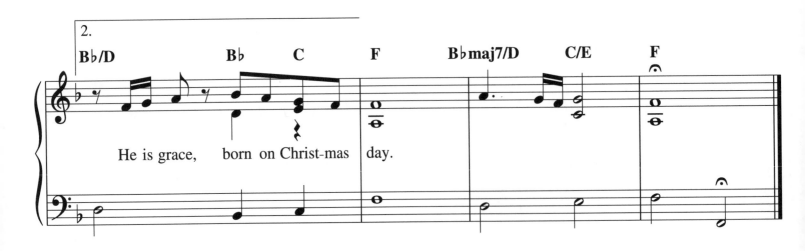

He is grace, born on Christ-mas day.

JINGLE-BELL ROCK

Words and Music by JOE BEAL
and JIM BOOTHE

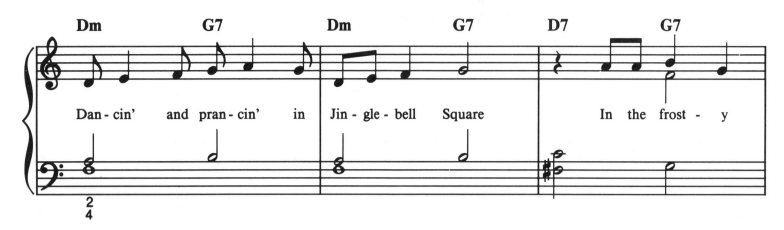

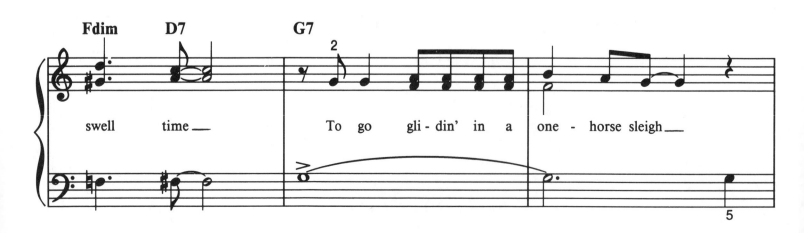

119

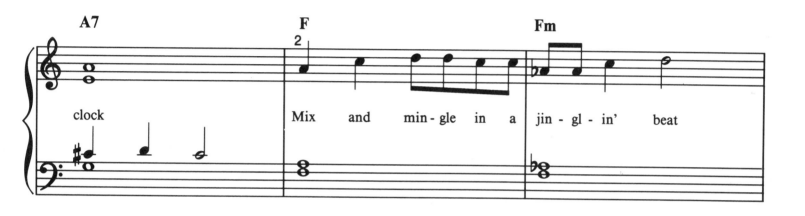

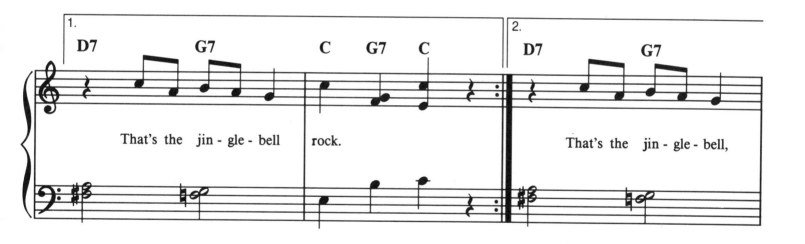

JINGLE BELLS

Words and Music by
J. PIERPONT

Brightly

With pedal

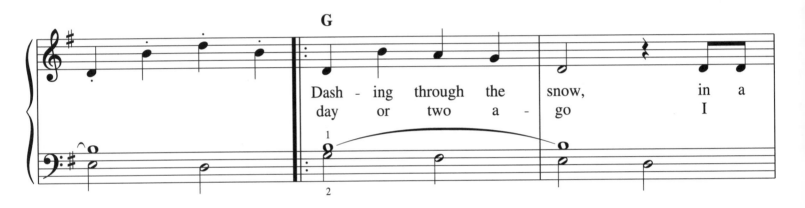

Dash - ing through the snow, in a
day or two a - go I

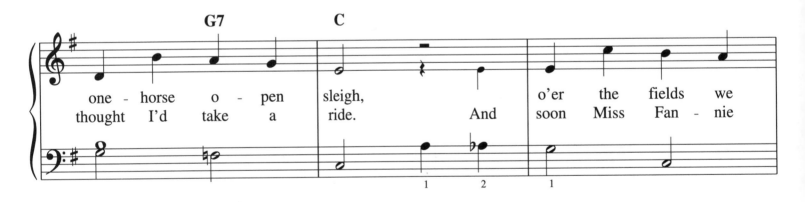

one - horse o - pen sleigh, And o'er the fields we
thought I'd take a ride. soon Miss Fan - nie

go laugh - ing all the way. The
Bright was seat - ed by my side.

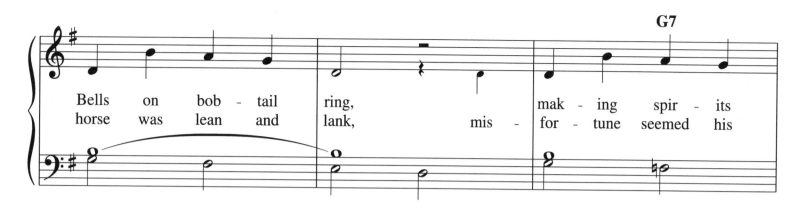

Bells on bob - tail ring, mak - ing spir - its
horse was lean and lank, mis - for - tune seemed his

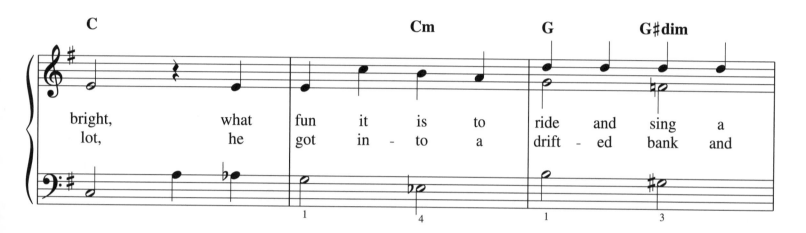

bright, what fun it is to ride and sing a
lot, what he got in - to a drift - ed bank and

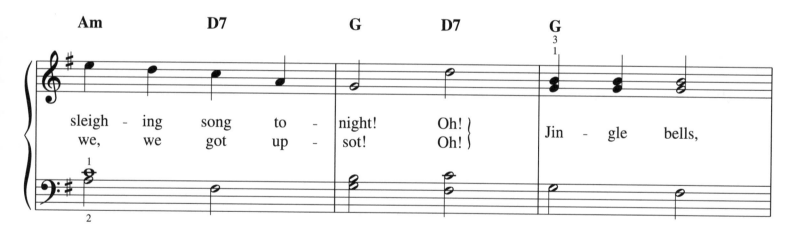

sleigh - ing song to - night! Oh! Jin - gle bells,
we, we got up - sot! Oh!

jin - gle bells, jin - gle all the way.

122

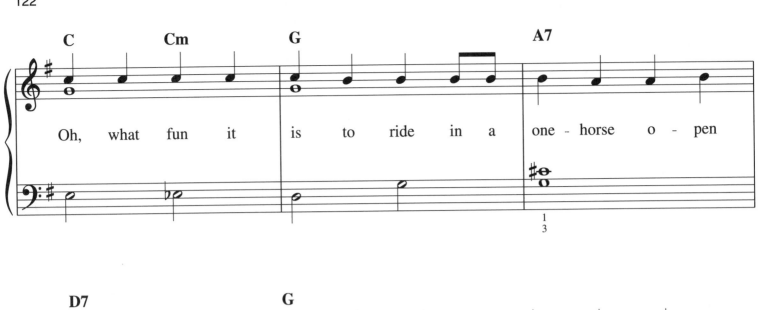

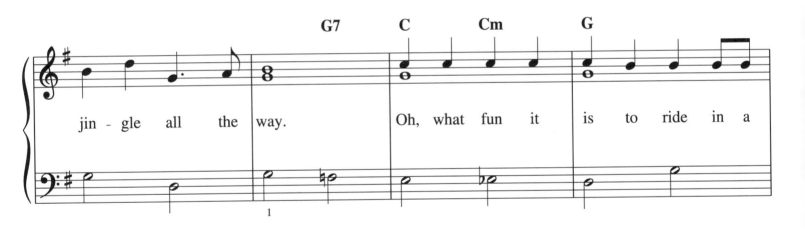

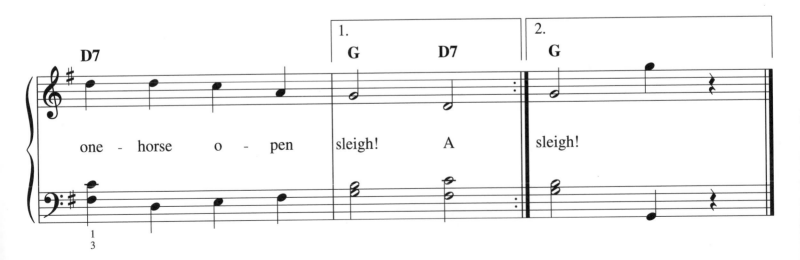

JINGLE, JINGLE, JINGLE

Music and Lyrics by
JOHNNY MARKS

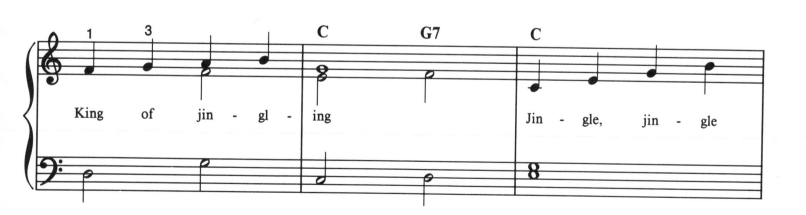

rein - deer, through the frost - y air they'll go,

They are not just plain deer, they're the fast - est deer I

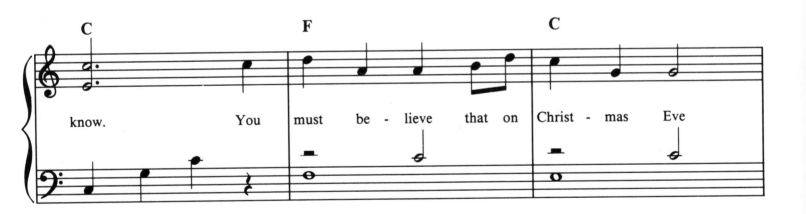

know. You must be - lieve that on Christ - mas Eve

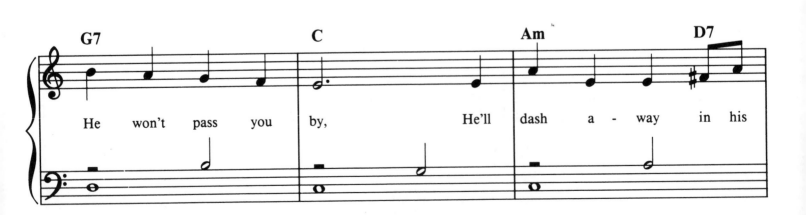

He won't pass you by, He'll dash a - way in his

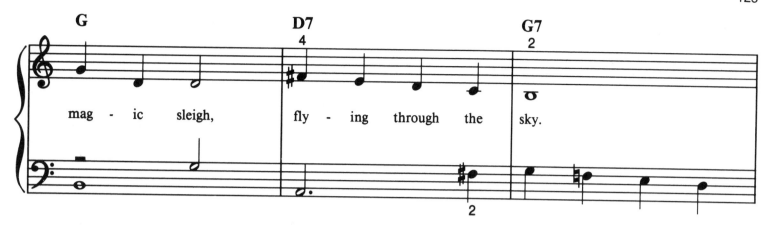

mag - ic sleigh, fly - ing through the sky.

Jin - gle, jin - gle, jin - gle, you will hear his sleigh bells

ring, Jol - ly old Kris Krin - gle is the

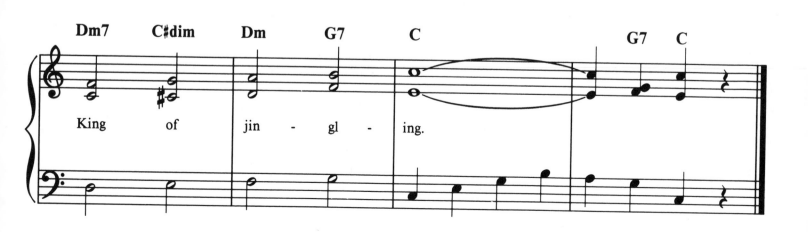

King of jin - gl - ing.

JOLLY OLD ST. NICHOLAS

Traditional 19th Century American Carol

127

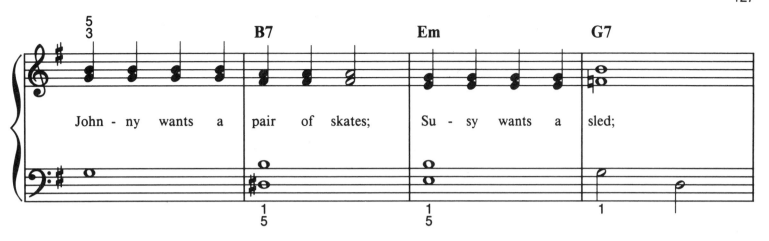

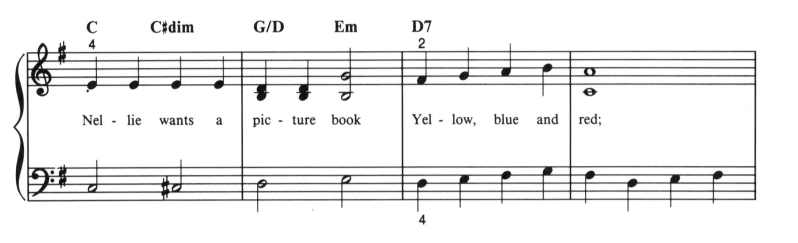

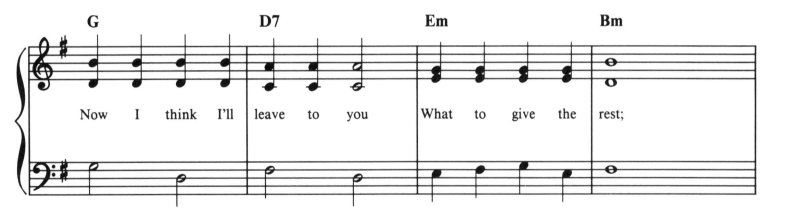

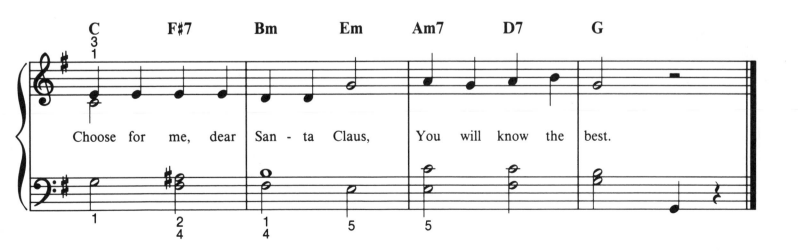

JOY TO THE WORLD

Words by ISAAC WATTS
Music by GEORGE FRIDERIC HANDEL

THE LAST MONTH OF THE YEAR
(What Month Was Jesus Born In?)

Words and Music by
VERA HALL
Adapted and Arranged by RUBY PICKENS TARTT
and ALAN LOMAX

Moderately

What month was my Je - sus born in? Last month of the year!

What month was my Je - sus born in? Last month of the year! Oh,

Jan - u - ar - y, (Jan - u - ar - y) Feb - ru - ar - y, (Feb - ru - ar - y) March,

131

Verse 2:
Well, they laid Him in a manger,....

Chorus:
Oh, January, February, March, April, May, June,
O Lord, you got July, August, September, October and-a November,
On the twenty fifth day of December
In the last month of the year.

Verse 3:
Wrapped Him up in swaddling clothing,....

Chorus

Verse 4:
He was born of the Virgin Mary,....

Chorus

LET IT SNOW! LET IT SNOW! LET IT SNOW!

Words by SAMMY CAHN
Music by JULE STYNE

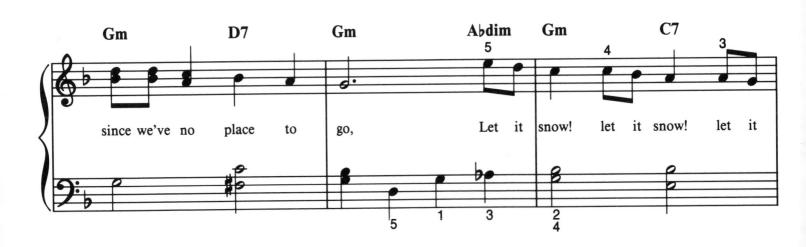

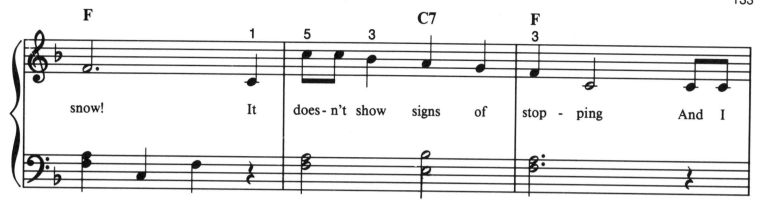

snow! It does-n't show signs of stop - ping And I

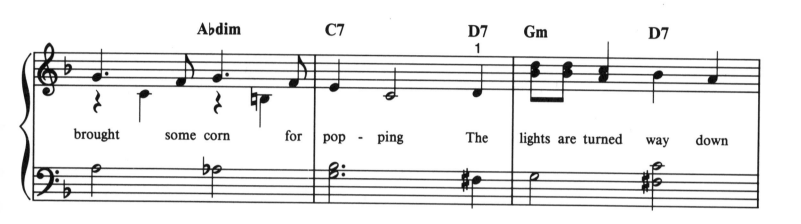

brought some corn for pop - ping The lights are turned way down

low, Let it snow! let it snow! let it snow! When we

fin - al - ly kiss good - night, How I'll hate go - ing out in the

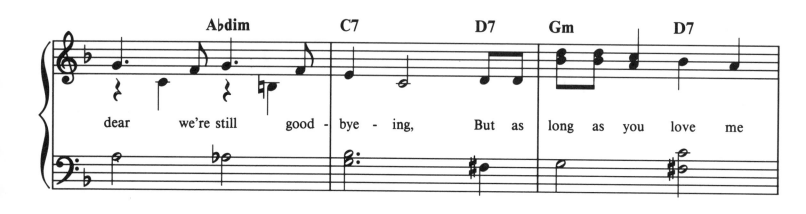

LO, HOW A ROSE
E'ER BLOOMING

15th Century German Carol
Translated by THEODORE BAKER
Music from *Alte Catholische Geistliche Kirchengesang*

136

LITTLE SAINT NICK

Words and Music by BRIAN WILSON
and MIKE LOVE

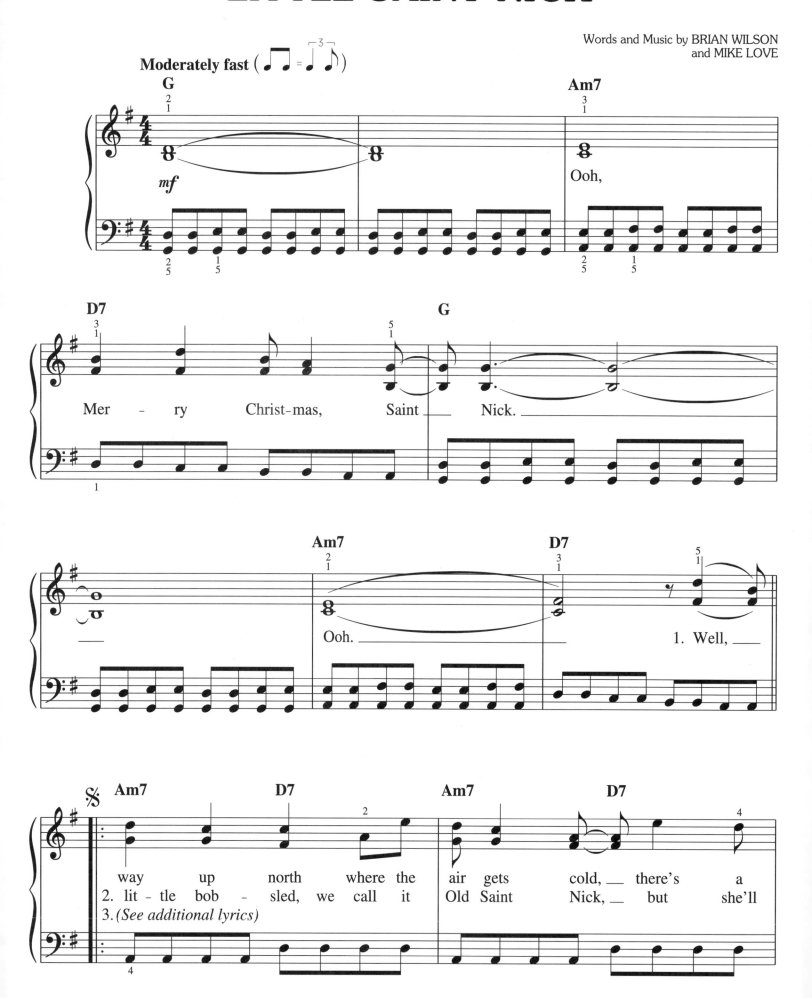

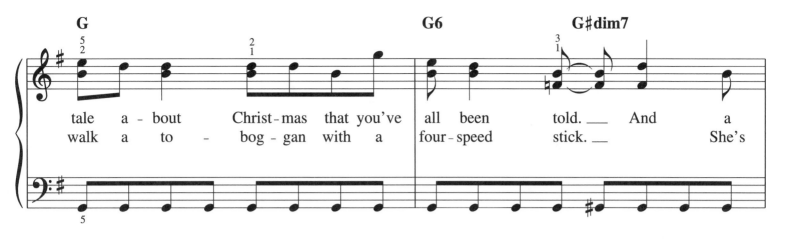

tale a - bout Christ-mas that you've all been told. ___ And a
walk a to - bog - gan with a four - speed stick. ___ She's

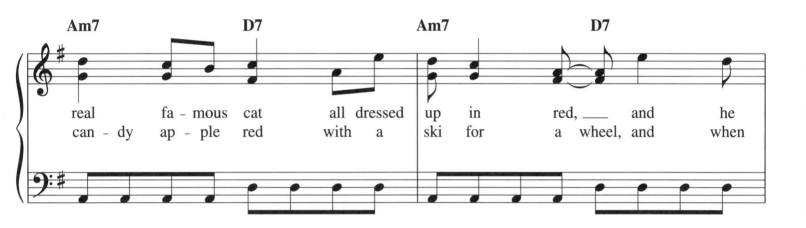

real fa - mous cat all dressed up in red, ___ and he
can - dy ap - ple red with a ski for a wheel, and when

spends the whole ___ year work - in' out on his sled. ___ } It's the
San - ta hits the gas, man, just watch her ___ peel. ___

To Coda ⊕

Lit - tle Saint Nick. (Lit - tle Saint Nick.) ___ It's the

Additional Lyrics

3. Haulin' through the snow at a fright'nin' speed,
   With a half a dozen deer with Rudy to lead,
   He's gotta wear his goggles 'cause the snow really flies,
   And he's cruisin' ev'ry pad with a little surprise.

A MARSHMALLOW WORLD

Words by CARL SIGMAN
Music by PETER DE ROSE

Moderately

mf

It's a marsh-mal-low world in the win-ter_____ When the

snow comes to cov-er the ground. It's the time for play___ It's a

whipped cream day___ I wait for it the whole year round. Those are

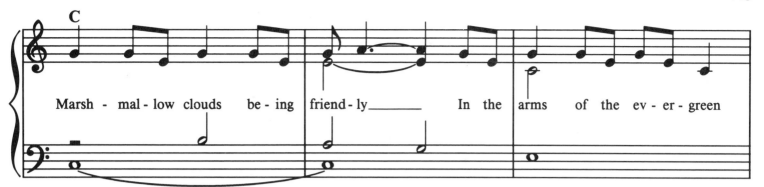

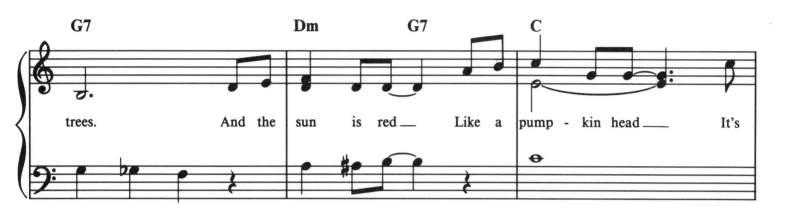

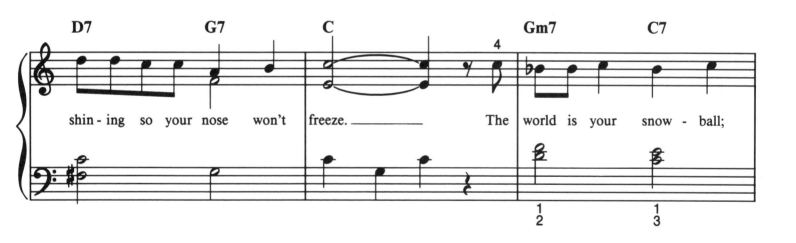

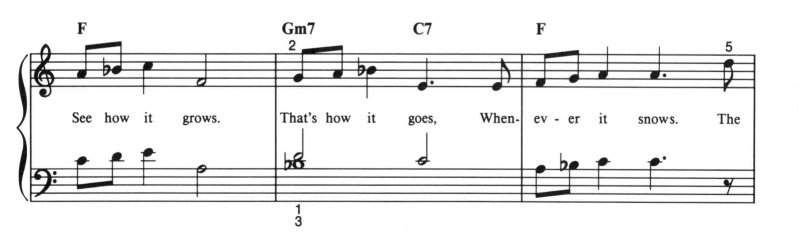

144

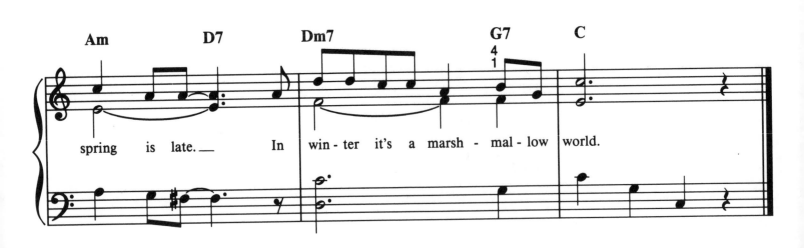

MARY'S LITTLE BOY CHILD

Words and Music by
JESTER HAIRSTON

man will live for - ev - er - more Be - cause of Christ - mas

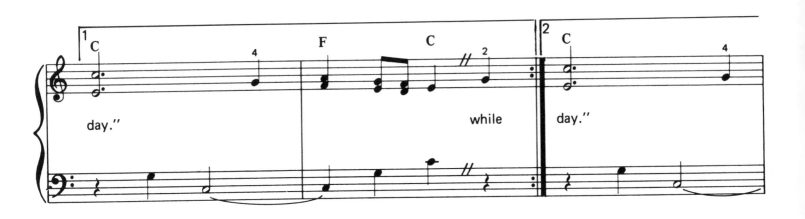

day." while day."

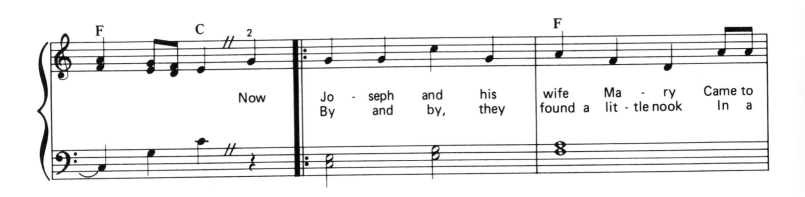

Now Jo - seph and his wife Ma - ry Came to
By and by, they found a lit - tle nook In a

Beth - le - hem that night; They
sta - ble all that for - lorn, And found no place to
found in a man - ger

147

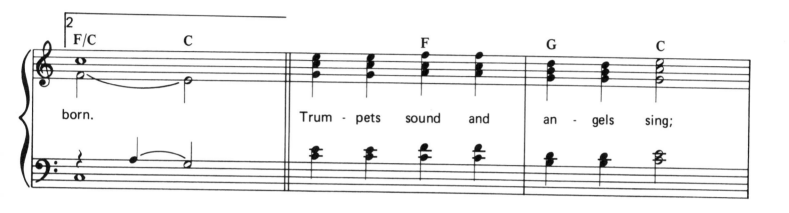

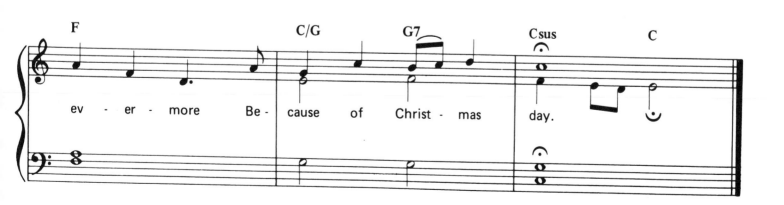

MERRY CHRISTMAS, DARLING

Words and Music by RICHARD CARPENTER
and FRANK POOLER

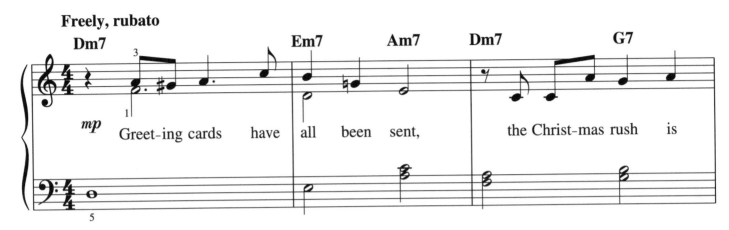

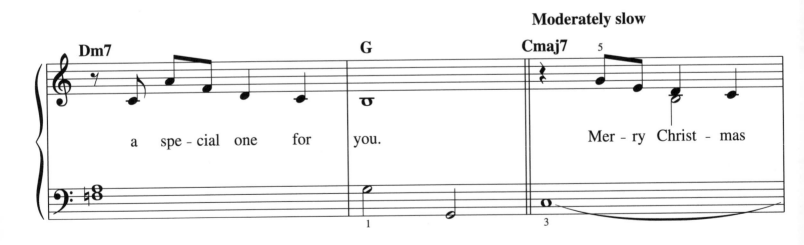

150

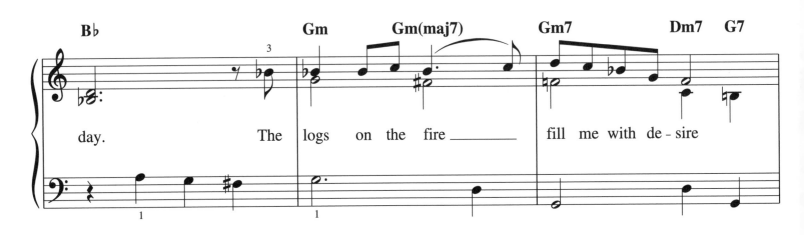

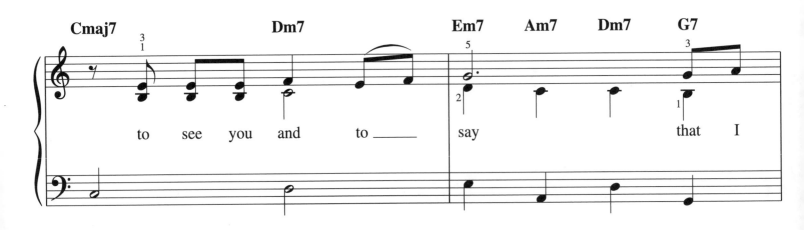

MERRY CHRISTMAS FROM THE FAMILY

Words and Music by
ROBERT EARL KEEN

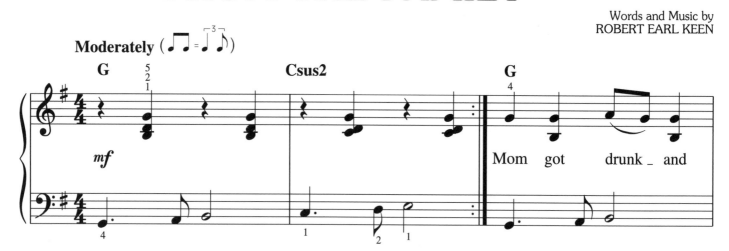

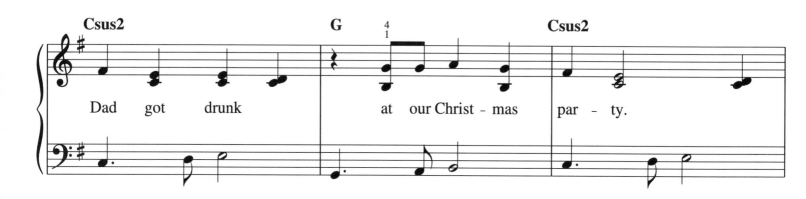

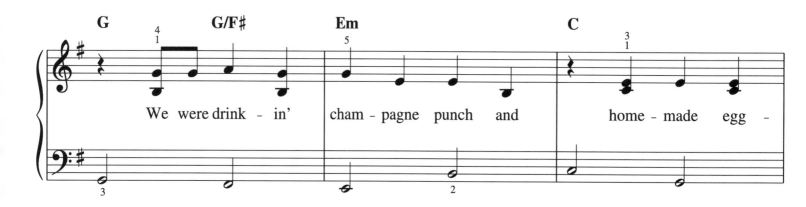

153

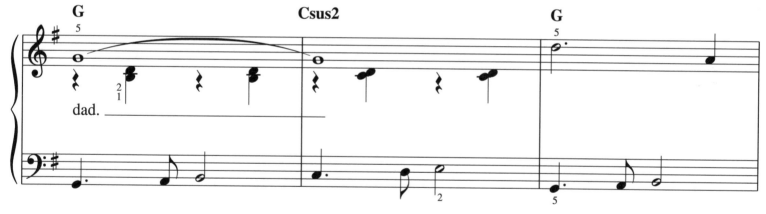

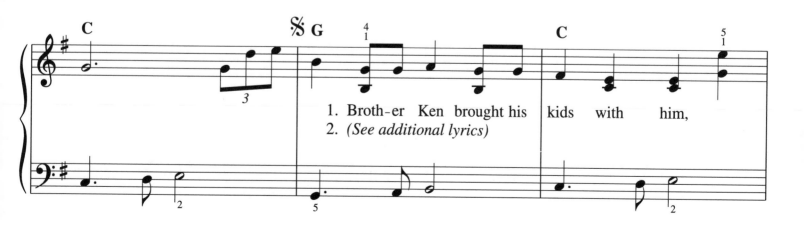

the three from his first wife Lynn, and the two i-

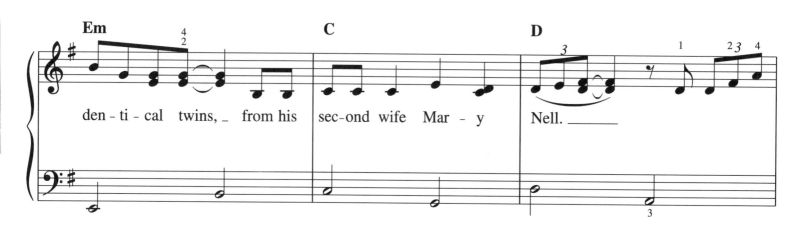

den - ti - cal twins, _ from his sec-ond wife Mar - y Nell. _____

'Course he brought his new wife Kaye, who talks all a -

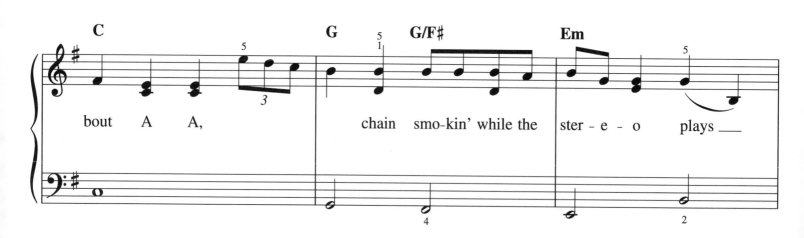

bout A A, chain smo-kin' while the ster - e - o plays ___

155

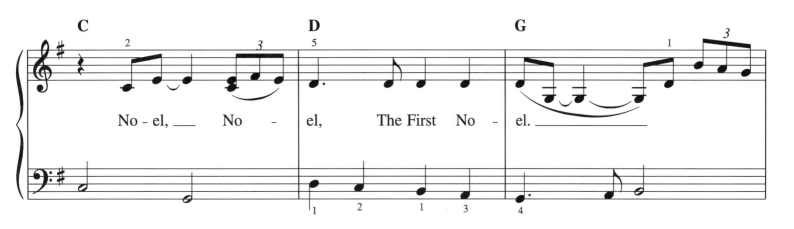

No - el, ___ No - el, The First No - el. ___

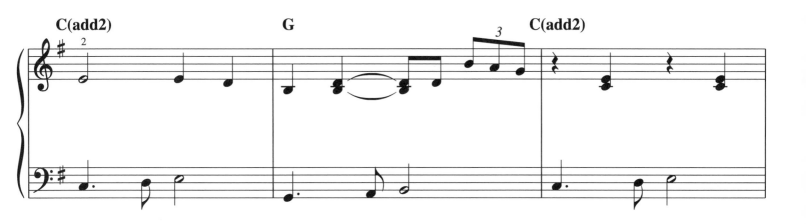

Chorus

Carve the tur-key, turn the ball game on, ___

{ mix mar - ga - ri - tas when the
make blood - y mar - ys 'cause we

{ egg-nog's gone. ___
all want one. ___

Send some-bod - y to the

{ Quick - pak store, ___
Stop 'N' Go, ___

156

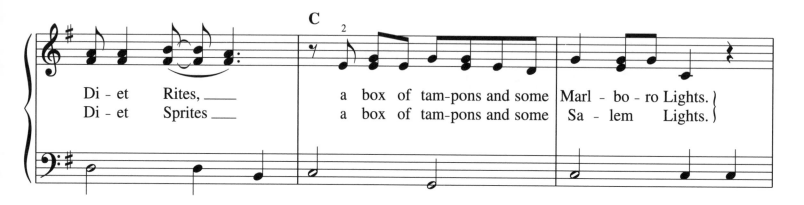

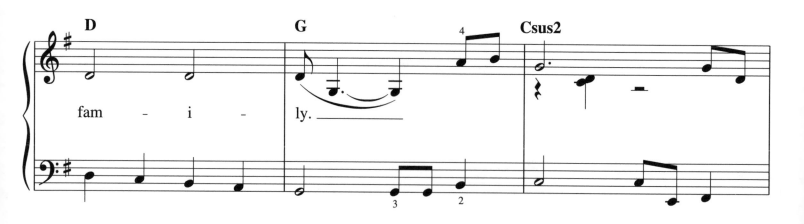

157

Additional Lyrics

2. Fran and Rita drove from Harlingen.
   I can't remember how I'm kin to them.
   But when they tried to plug their motor home in,
   They blew our Christmas lights.
   Cousin David knew just what went wrong,
   So we all waited out on our front lawn.
   He threw the breaker and the lights came on
   And we sang Silent Night,
   O, Silent Night.
   Chorus

THE MERRY CHRISTMAS POLKA

Words by PAUL FRANCIS WEBSTER
Music by SONNY BURKE

Moderately (in 2)

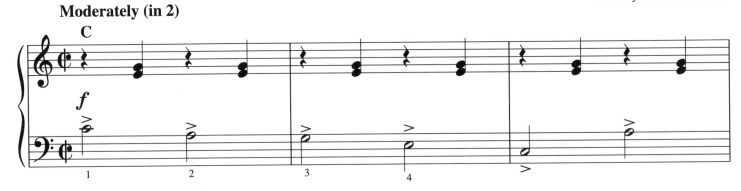

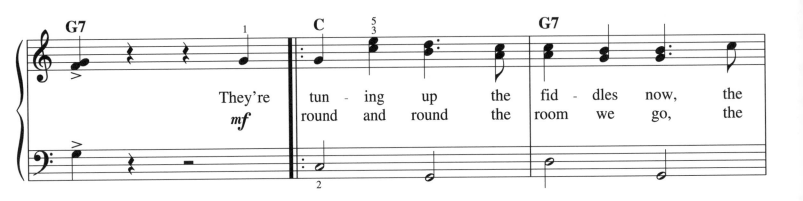

They're / round and round the
tun - ing up the fid - dles now, the
room we go, the

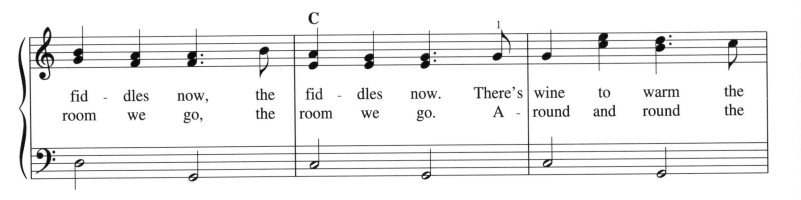

fid - dles now, the fid - dles now. There's wine to warm the
room we go, the room we go. A - round and round the

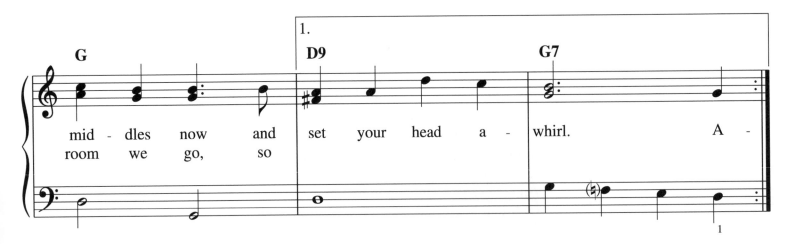

mid - dles now and set your head a - whirl. A -
room we go, and so

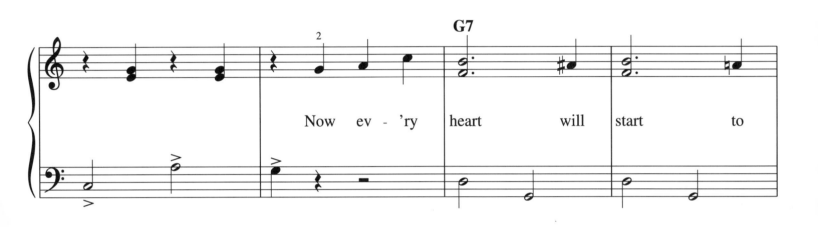

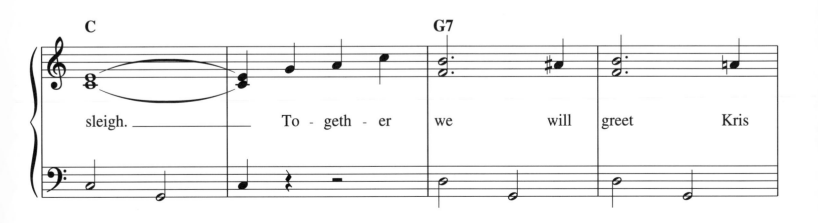

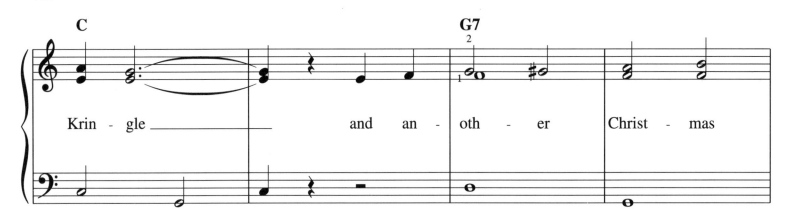

C

G7

Krin - gle _____ and an - oth - er Christ - mas

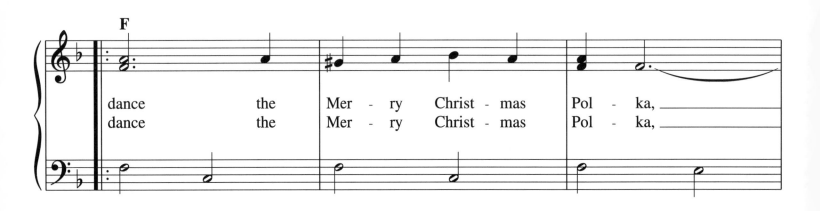

C7

Day. _____ Come on and

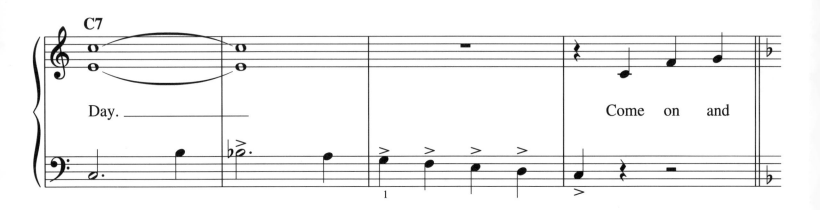

F

dance the Mer - ry Christ - mas Pol - ka, _____
dance the Mer - ry Christ - mas Pol - ka, _____

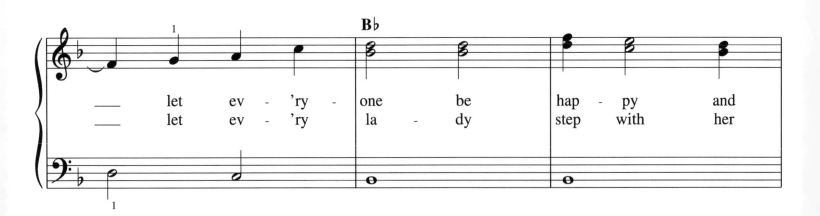

B♭

___ let ev - 'ry - one be hap - py and
___ let ev - 'ry la - dy step with her

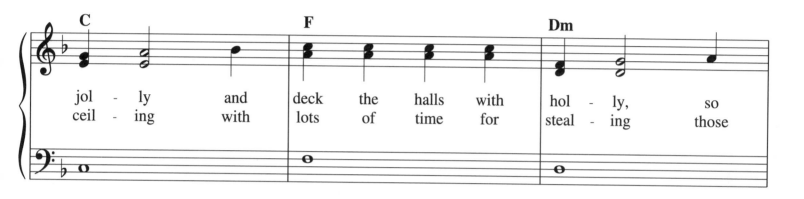

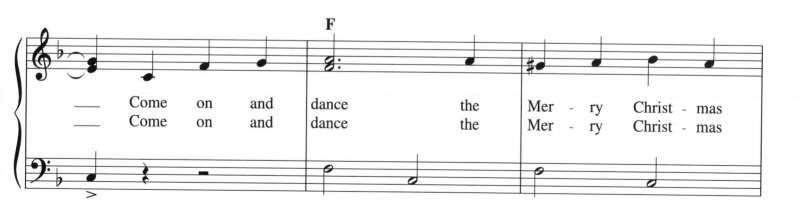

162

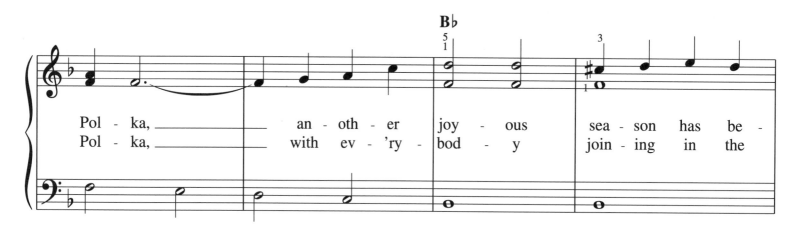

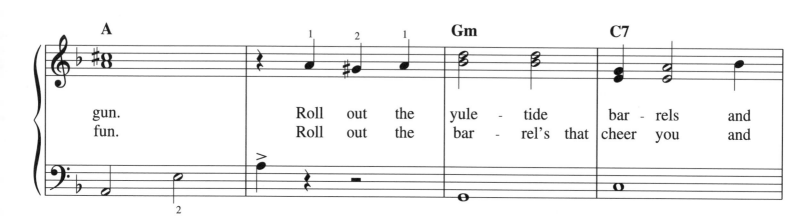

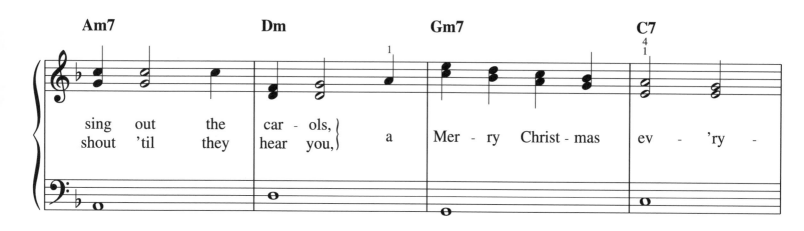

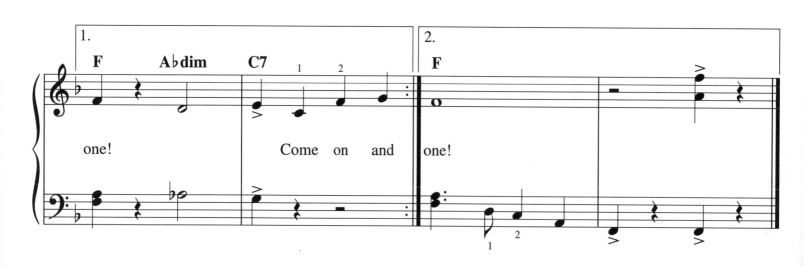

A MERRY, MERRY CHRISTMAS TO YOU

Music and Lyrics by
JOHNNY MARKS

THE MOST WONDERFUL DAY OF THE YEAR

Music and Lyrics by
JOHNNY MARKS

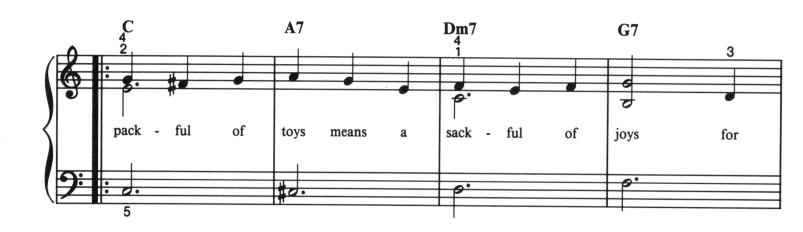

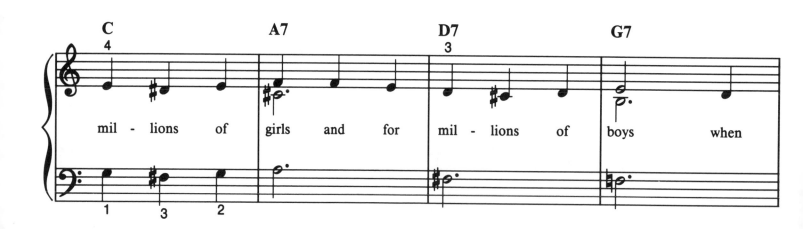

167

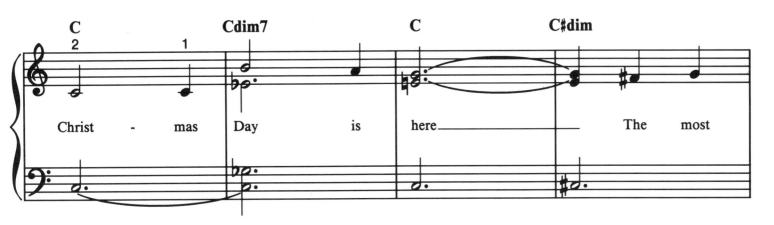

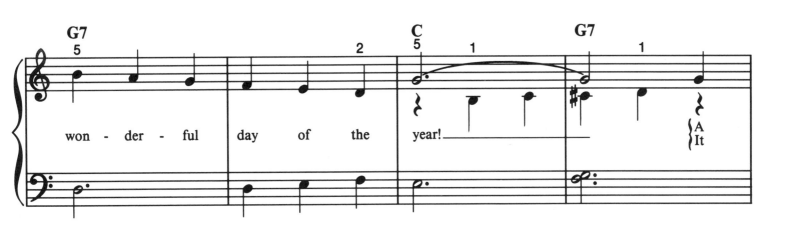

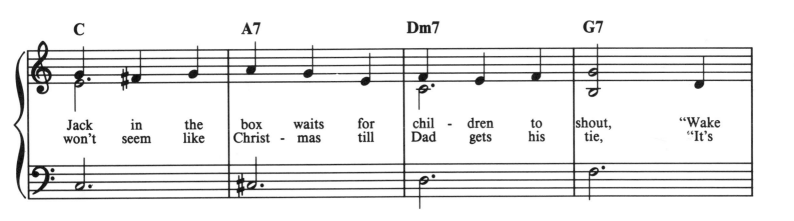

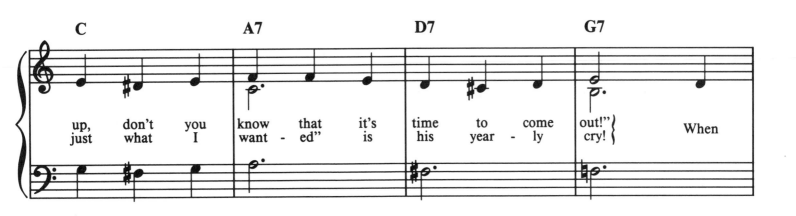

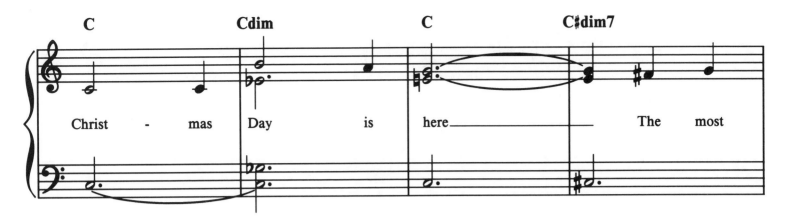

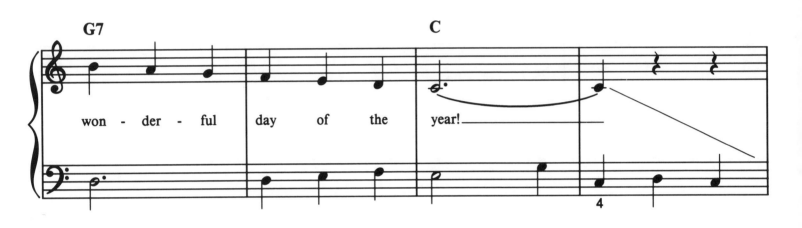

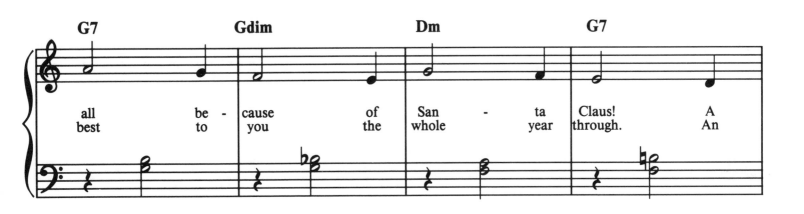

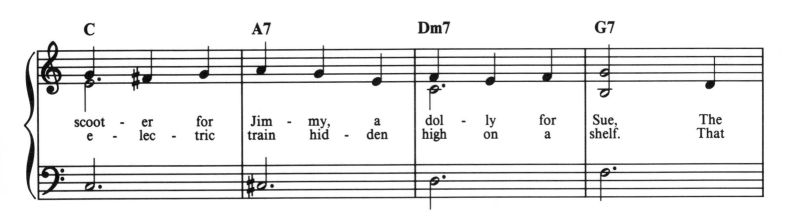

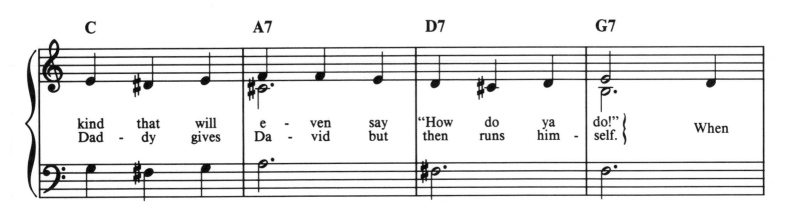

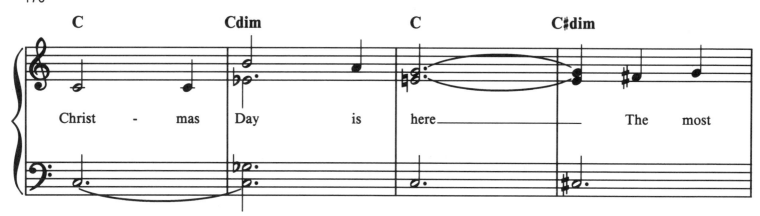

Christ - mas Day is here _____ The most

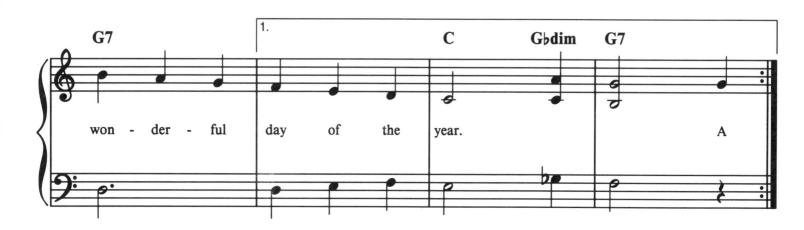

won - der - ful day of the year. A

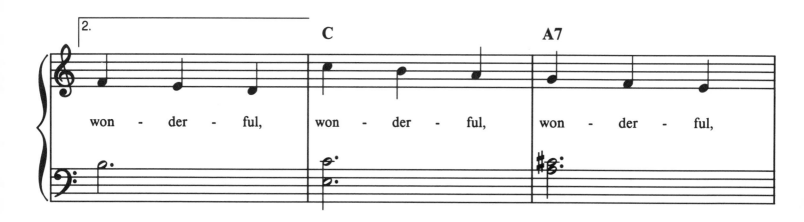

won - der - ful, won - der - ful, won - der - ful,

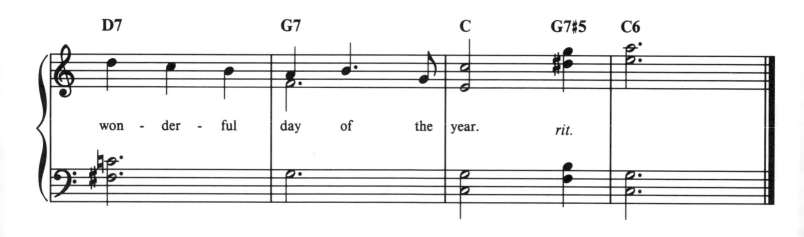

won - der - ful day of the year. *rit.*

O CHRISTMAS TREE

Traditional German Carol

MY FAVORITE THINGS
from THE SOUND OF MUSIC

Lyrics by OSCAR HAMMERSTEIN II
Music by RICHARD RODGERS

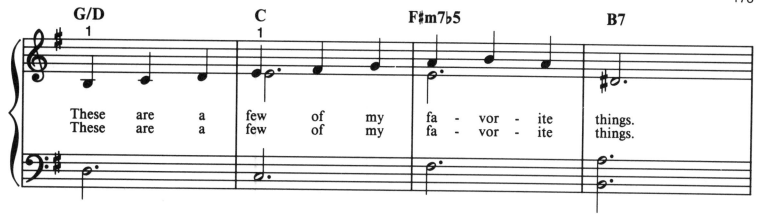

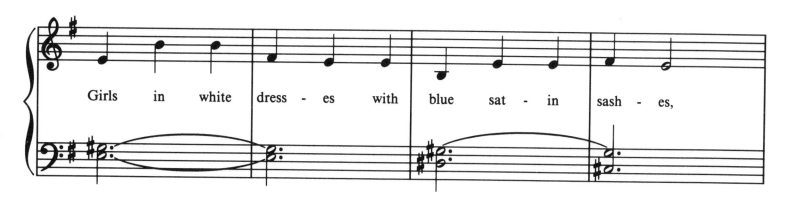

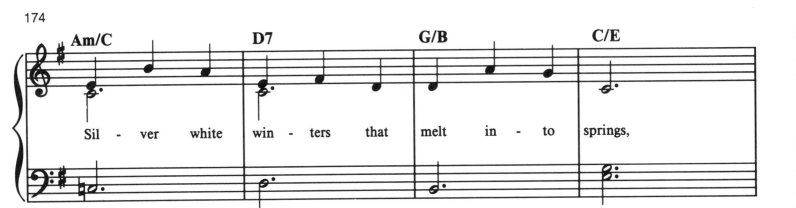

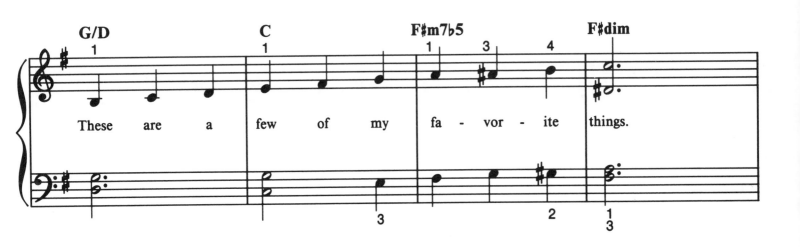

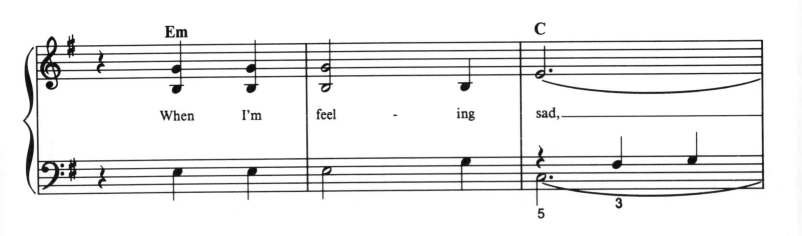

175

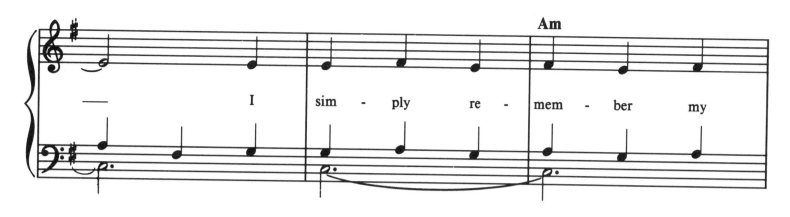

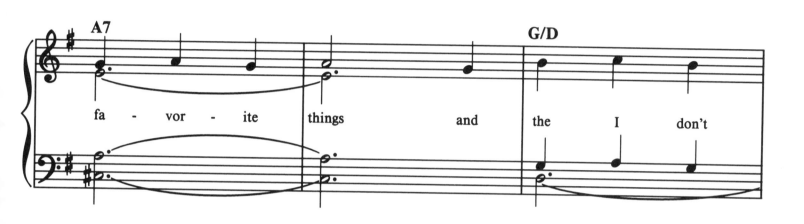

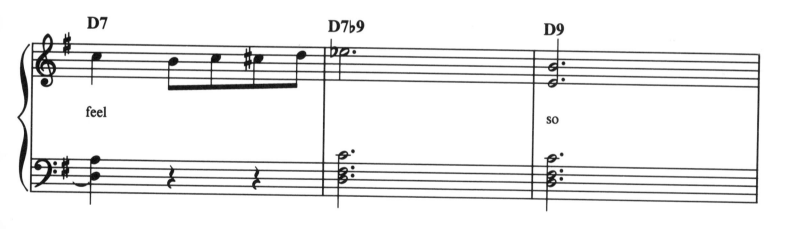

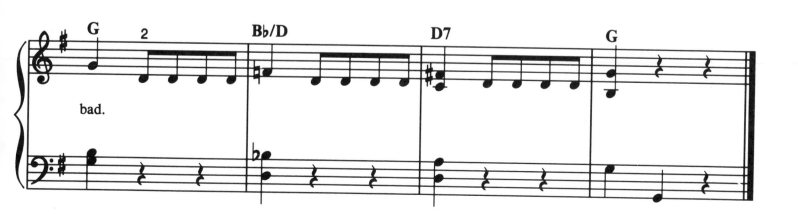

THE NIGHT BEFORE CHRISTMAS SONG

Music by JOHNNY MARKS
Lyrics adapted by JOHNNY MARKS
from CLEMENT MOORE'S Poem

177

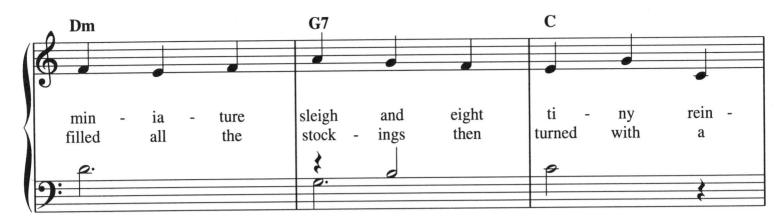

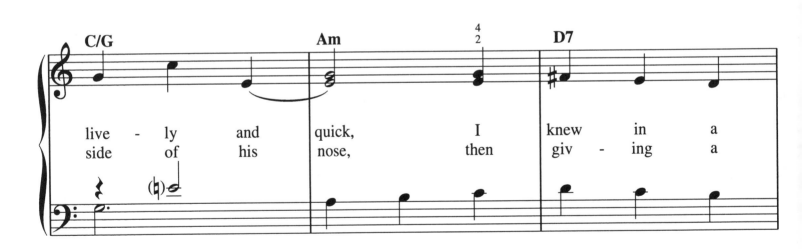

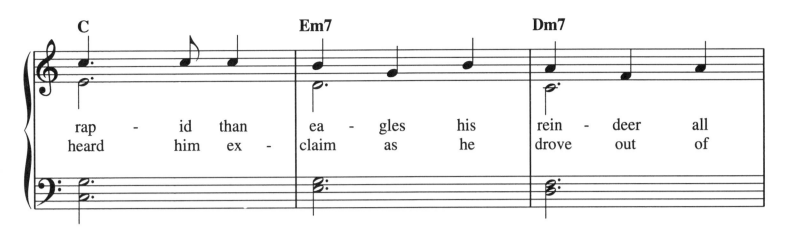

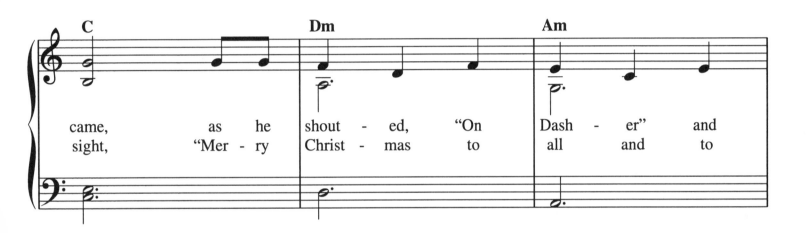

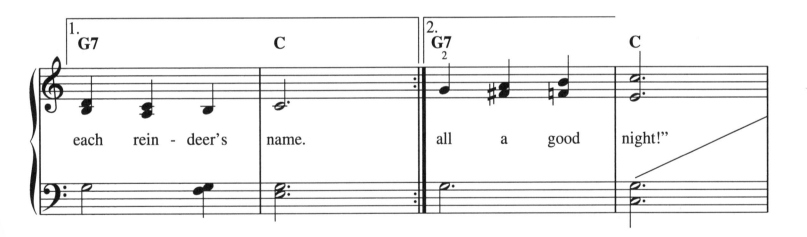

NOEL! NOEL!

French-English Carol

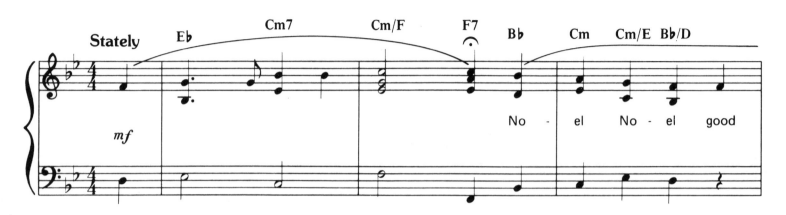

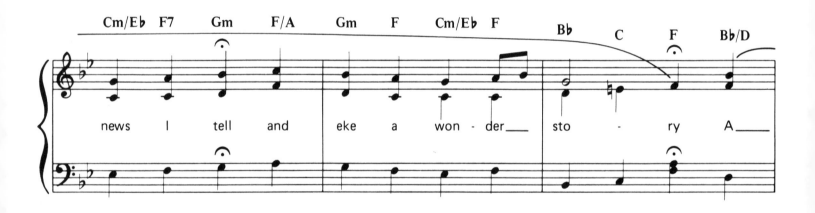

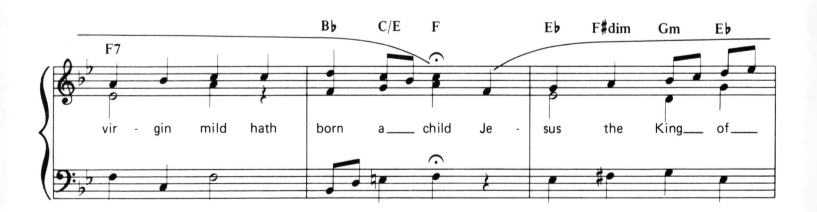

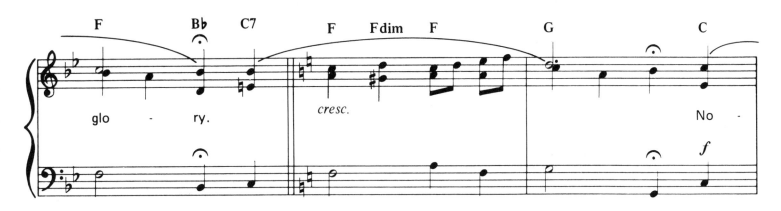

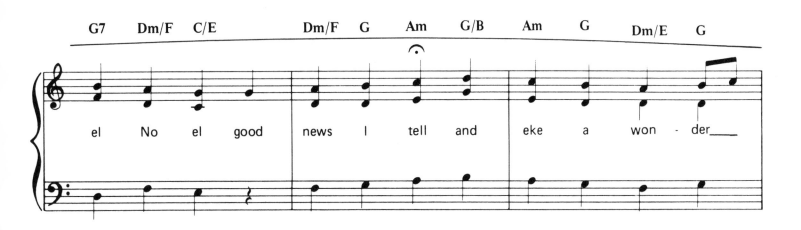

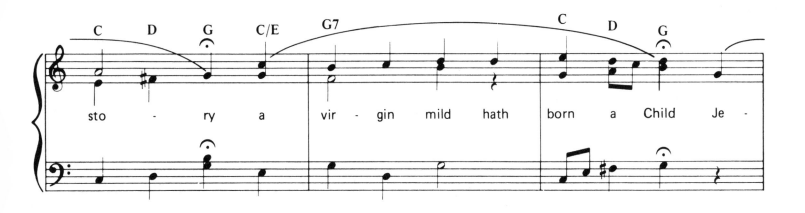

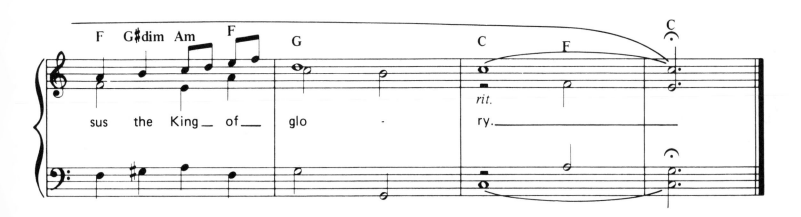

NUTTIN' FOR CHRISTMAS

Words and Music by ROY BENNETT
and SID TEPPER

Moderately fast

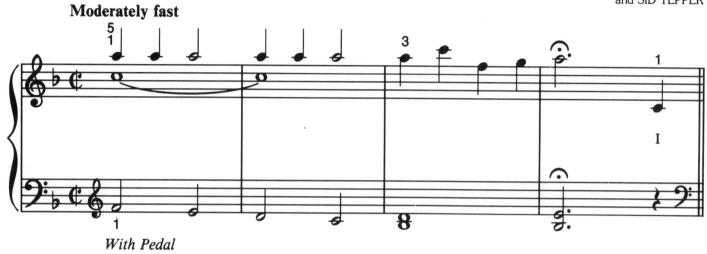

With Pedal

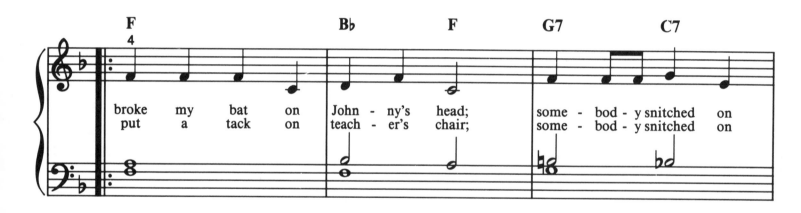

broke my bat on John - ny's head; some - bod - y snitched on
put a tack on teach - er's chair; some - bod - y snitched on

me.   I hid a frog in sis - ter's bed;
me.   I tied a knot in Su - sie's hair;

183

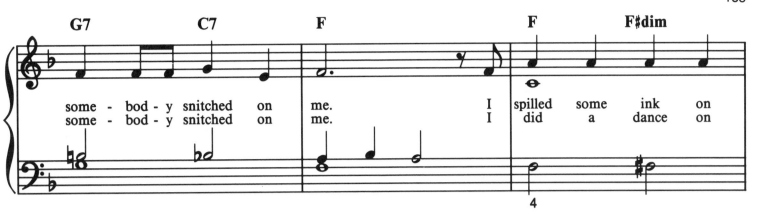

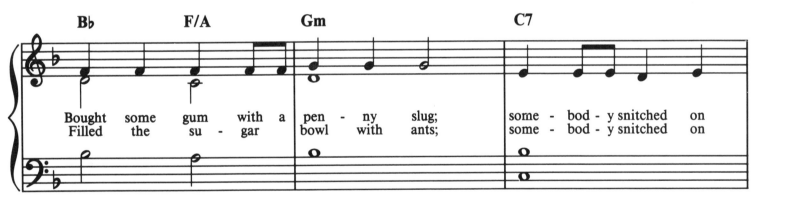

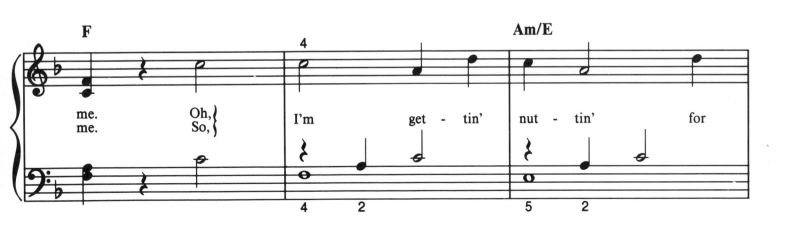

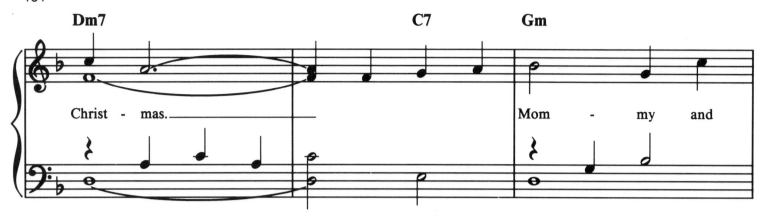

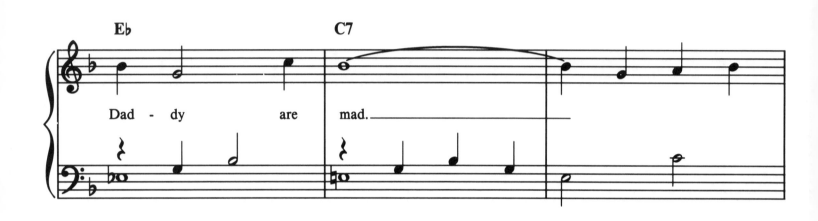

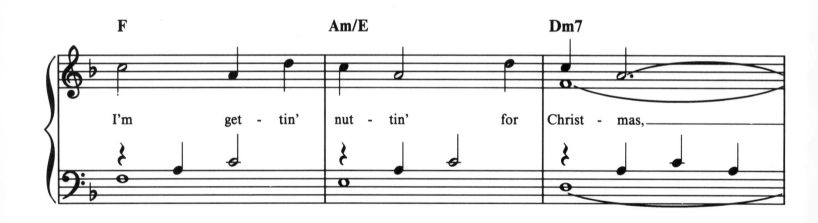

185

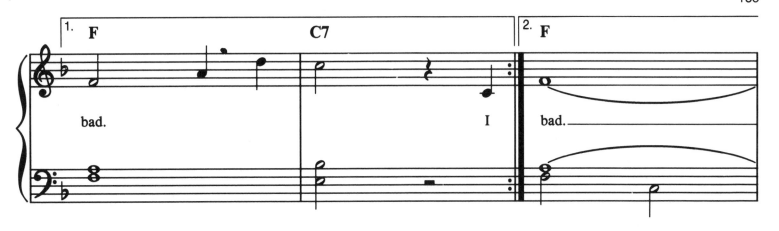

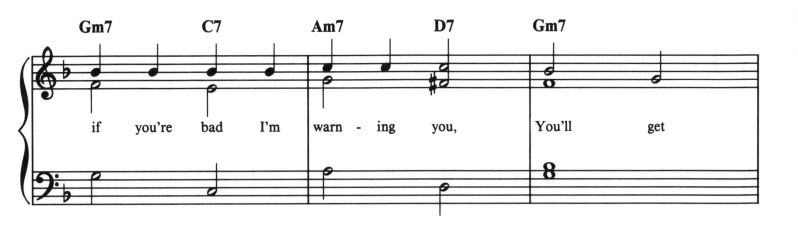

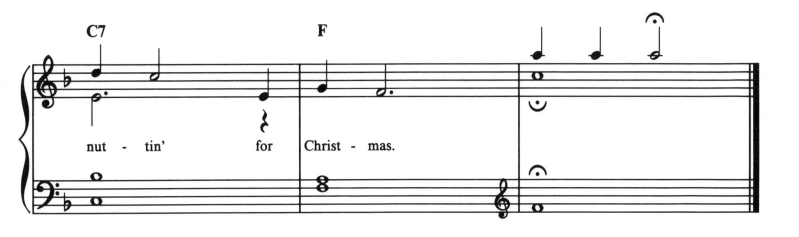

O COME, ALL YE FAITHFUL
(Adeste Fideles)

Words and Music by
JOHN FRANCIS WADE
Latin Words translated by FREDERICK OAKELEY

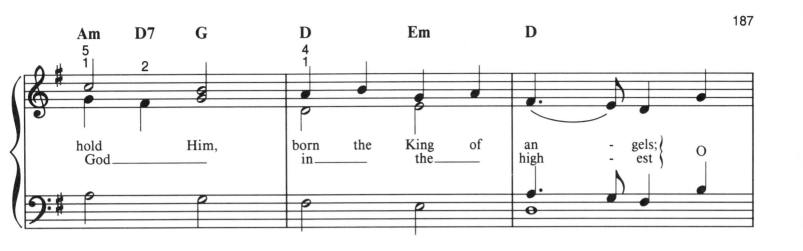

hold ___ Him, born the King of an - gels;} O
God ___ Him, in ___ the King the ___ high - est

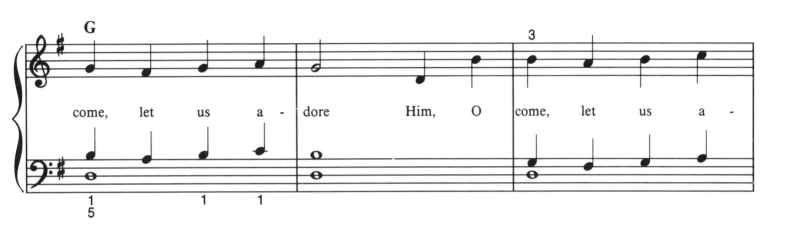

come, let us a - dore Him, O come, let us a -

dore Him, O come, let us a - dore Him, ___

Christ ___ the Lord! Lord!

O COME, LITTLE CHILDREN

Words by C. von SCHMIDT
Music by J.P.A. SCHULZ

Moderately fast

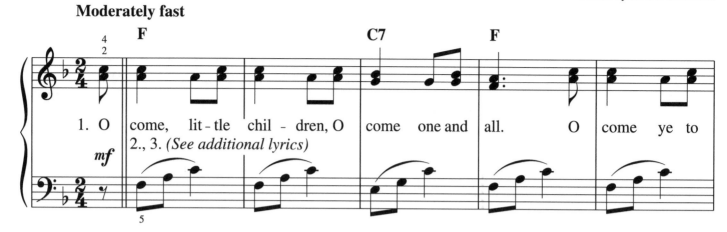

1. O come, lit-tle chil-dren, O come one and all. O come ye to

2., 3. *(See additional lyrics)*

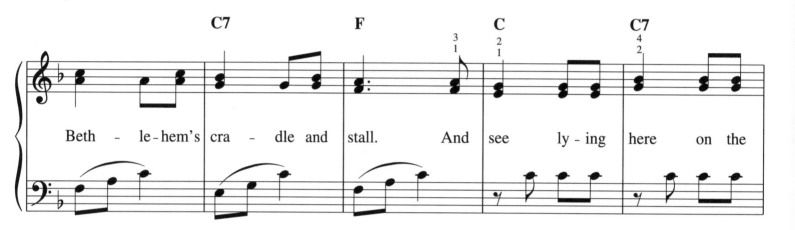

Beth - le-hem's cra - dle and stall. And see ly - ing here on the

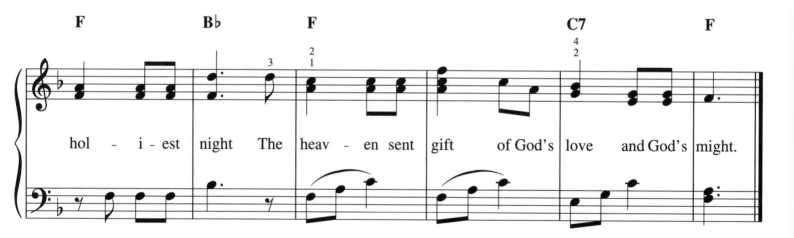

hol - i -est night The heav - en sent gift of God's love and God's might.

Additional Lyrics

2. The Baby lies here on the straw and the hay,
   While Joseph and Mary are kneeling to pray;
   The shepherds have hastened to worship their King,
   And angels in chorus right cheerfully sing.

3. We too would be humble and worship the Child
   With shepherds and Joseph and Mary so mild.
   Let voices ring out – for how could we be sad?
   Rejoice with the angels for tidings so glad.

O SANCTISSIMA

Sicilian Carol

190

O COME, O COME IMMANUEL

Plainsong, 13th Century
Words translated by JOHN M. NEALE
and HENRY S. COFFIN

191

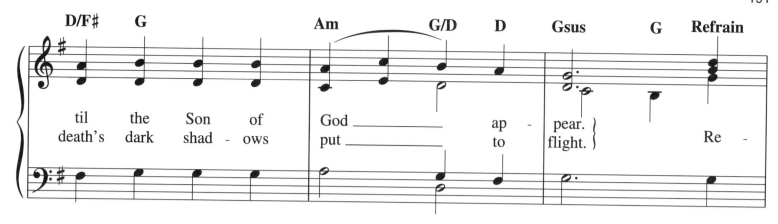

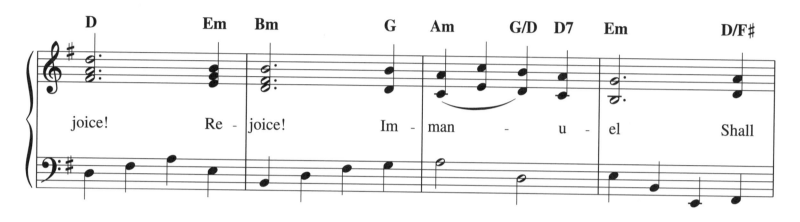

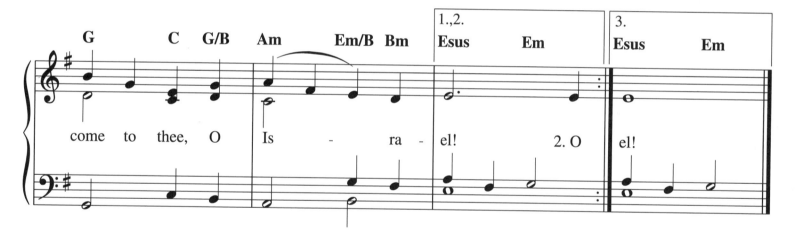

Additional Verses

3. O come, Thou wisdom from on high,
   And order all things, far and nigh;
   To us the path of knowledge show,
   And cause us in her ways to go.
   Refrain

4. O come, Desire of nations, bind
   All peoples in one heart and mind;
   Bid envy, strife and quarrels cease,
   Fill all the world with heaven's peace.
   Refrain

O HOLY NIGHT

French Words by PLACIDE CAPPEAU
English Words by JOHN S. DWIGHT
Music by ADOLPHE ADAM

Slow and flowing

mp

With pedal

O ho - ly night _____ the

stars are bright - ly shin - ing, it is the

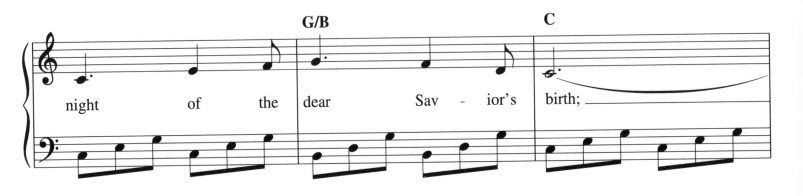

night of the dear Sav - ior's birth; _____

Long lay the world _____ in

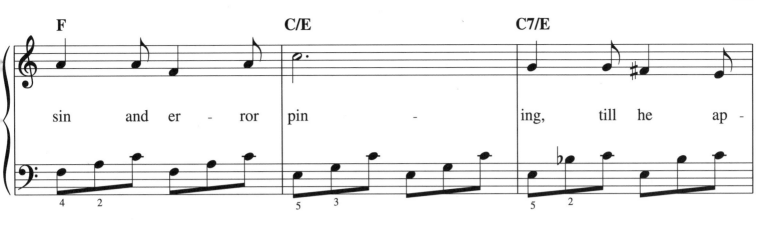

sin and er - ror pin - ing, till he ap -

peared and the soul felt its worth. _____

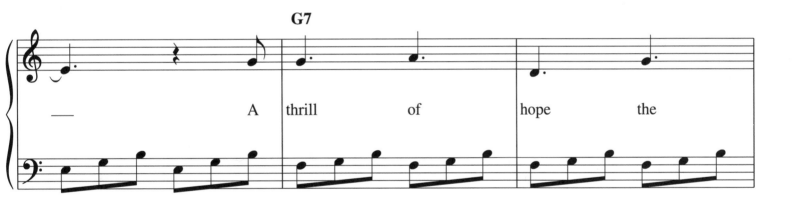

_____ A thrill of hope the

wea - ry soul re - joic - es, for yon - der

194

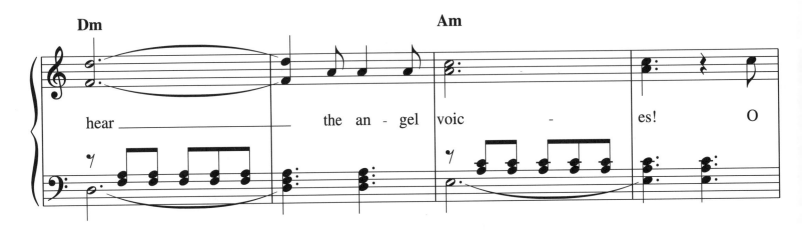

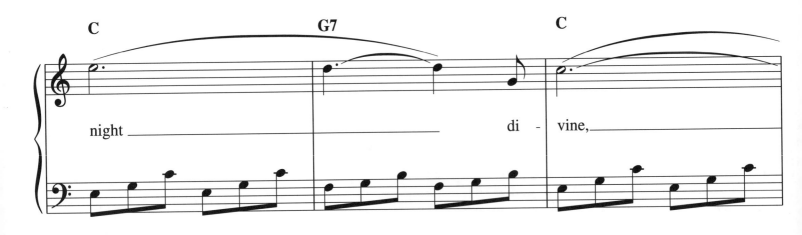

O night _____ when Christ was

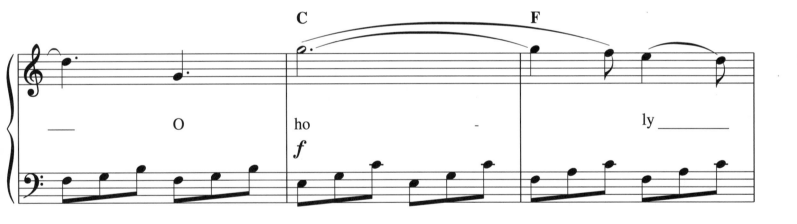

born. _____ O night, _____

cresc.

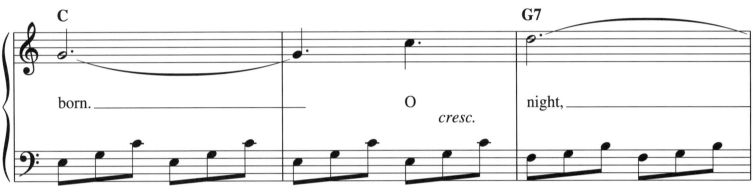

___ O ho - ly _____

f

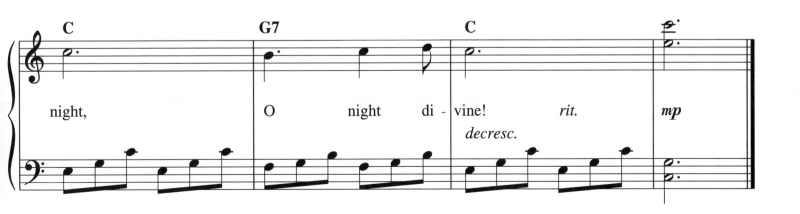

night, O night di - vine! *rit.* *mp*

decresc.

O LITTLE TOWN OF BETHLEHEM

Words by PHILLIPS BROOKS
Music by LEWIS H. REDNER

197

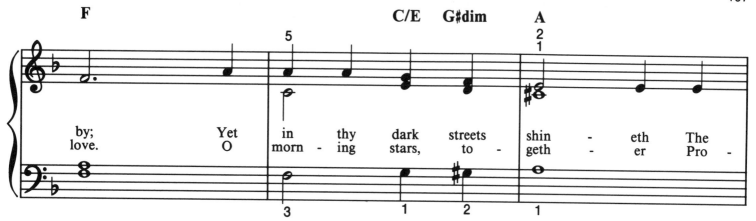

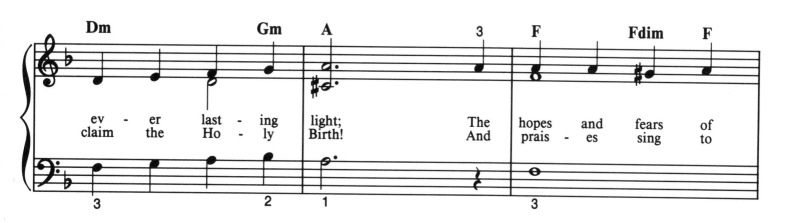

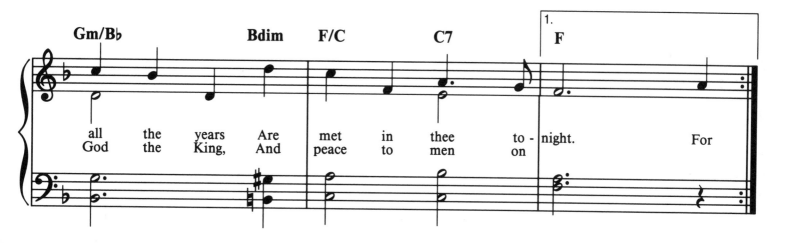

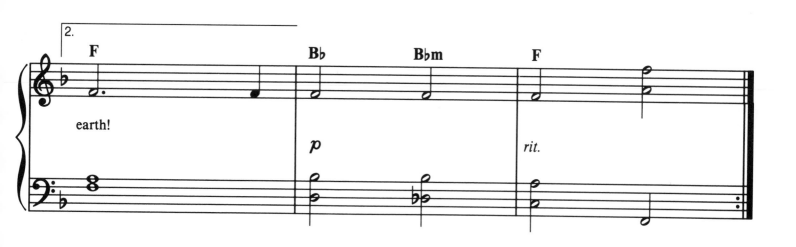

OLD TOY TRAINS

Words and Music by
ROGER MILLER

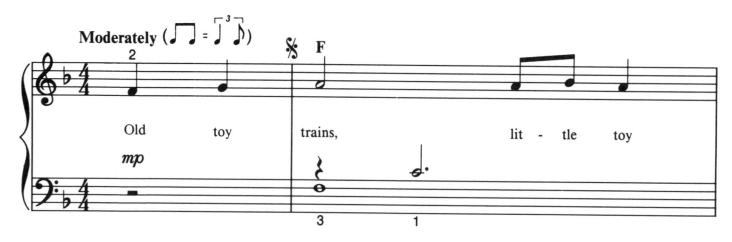

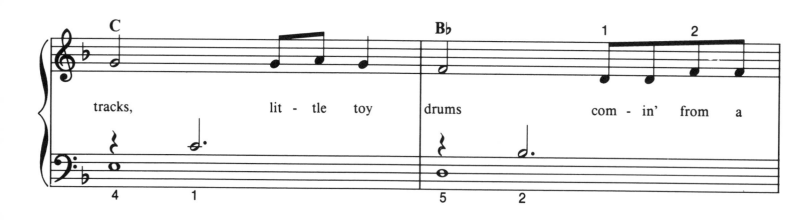

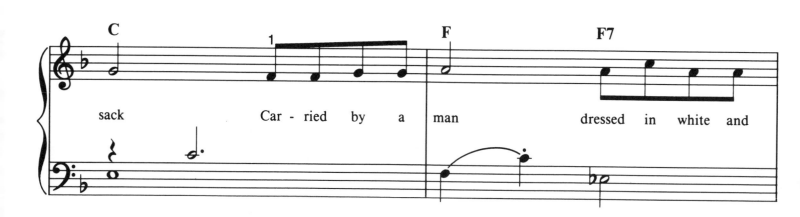

red; Lit - tle boy, don't you think it's time you were in

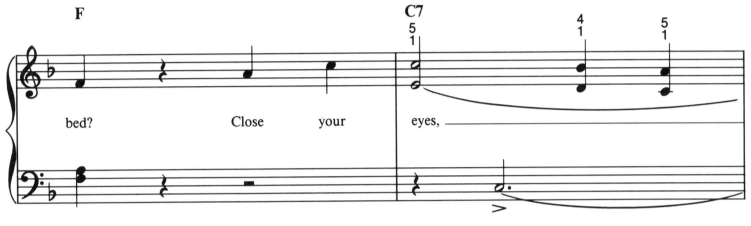

bed? Close your eyes,

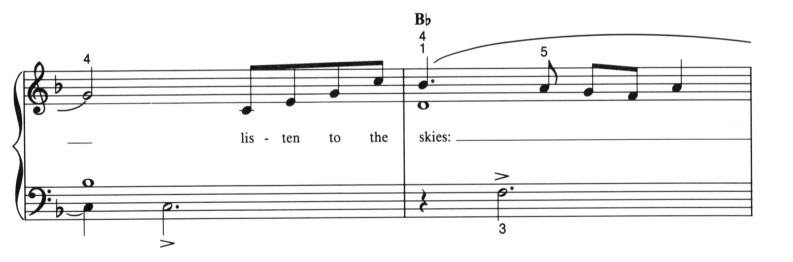

lis - ten to the skies:

All is calm, all is

200

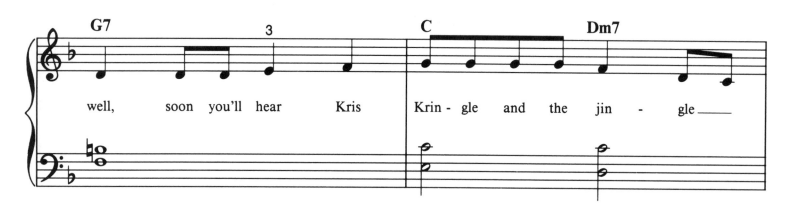

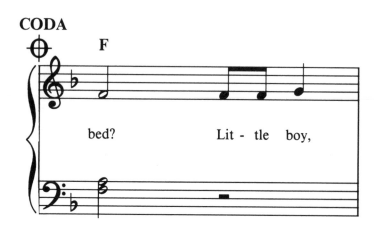

PRETTY PAPER

Words and Music by
WILLIE NELSON

Slowly, with expression

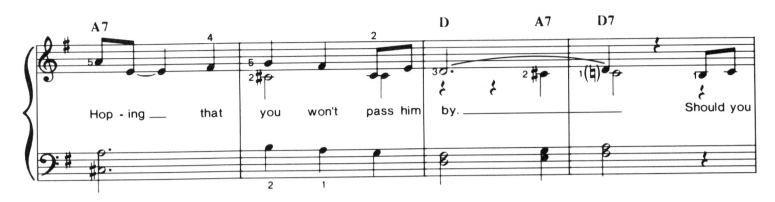

Hop - ing ___ that you won't pass him by. ___ Should you

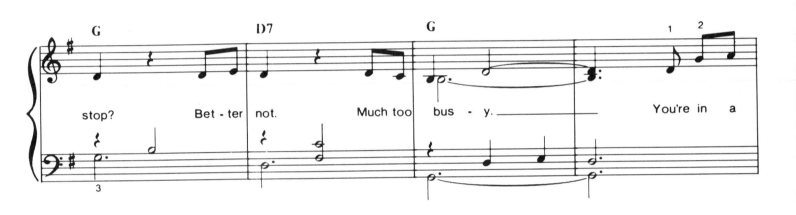

stop? Bet - ter not. Much too bus - y. ___ You're in a

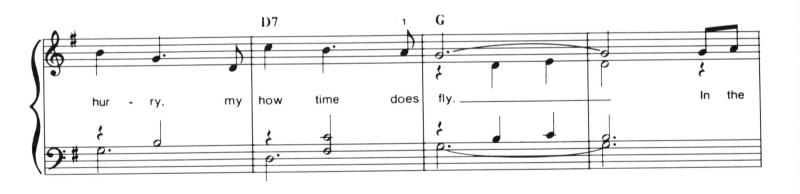

hur - ry, my how time does fly. ___ In the

dis - tance the ring - ing of ___ laugh - ter ___ And in the

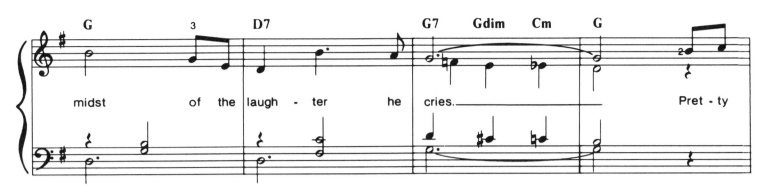

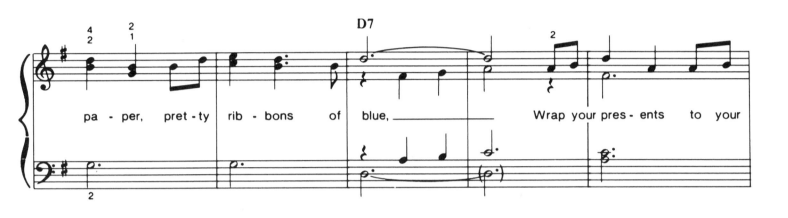

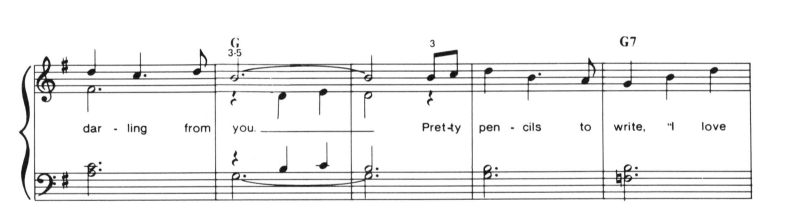

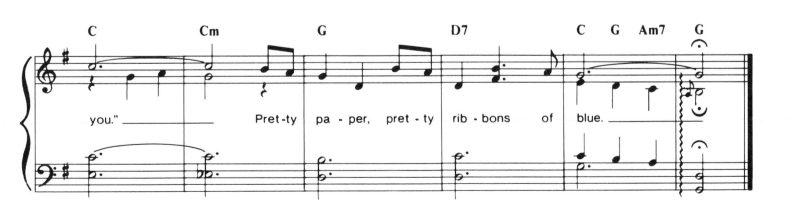

PARADE OF THE WOODEN SOLDIERS

English Lyrics by BALLARD MacDONALD
Music by LEON JESSEL

Slow March

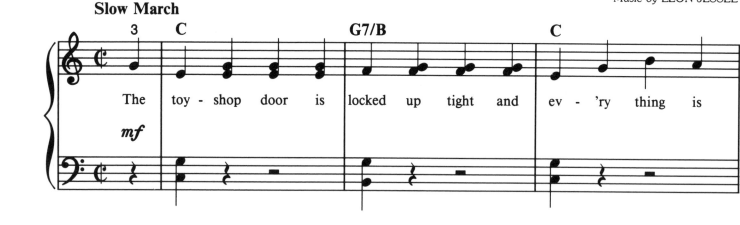

The toy-shop door is locked up tight and ev-'ry thing is

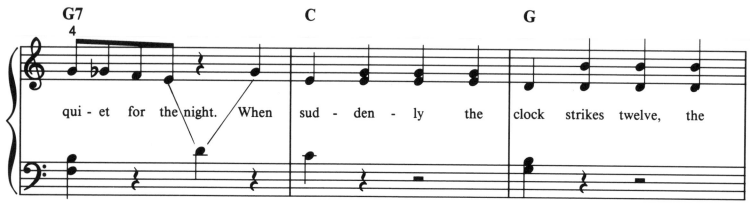

qui-et for the night. When sud-den-ly the clock strikes twelve, the

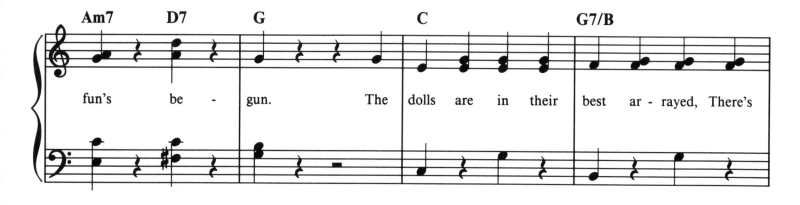

fun's be-gun. The dolls are in their best ar-rayed, There's

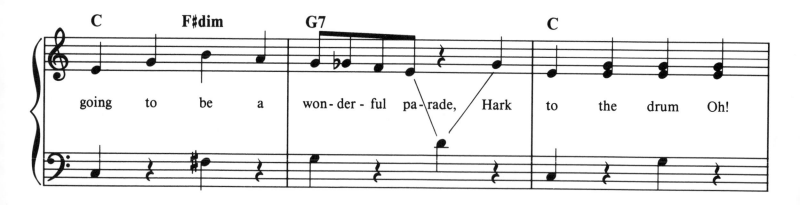

going to be a won-der-ful pa-rade, Hark to the drum Oh!

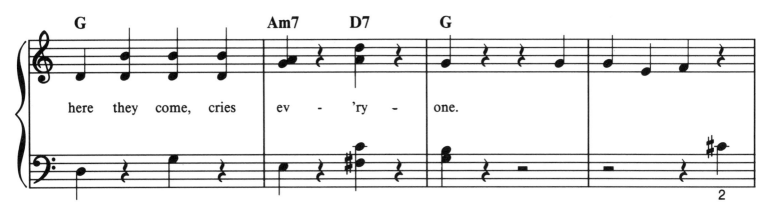

here they come, cries ev - 'ry - one.

Hear them all cheer - ing, Now they are near - ing,

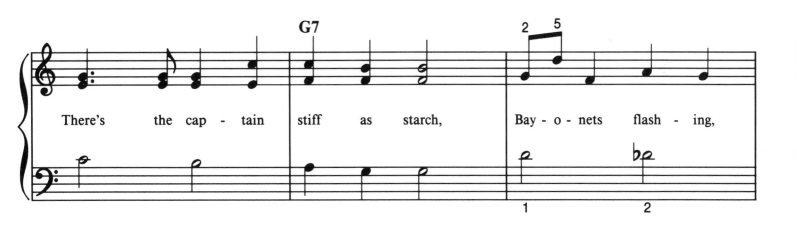

There's the cap - tain stiff as starch, Bay - o - nets flash - ing,

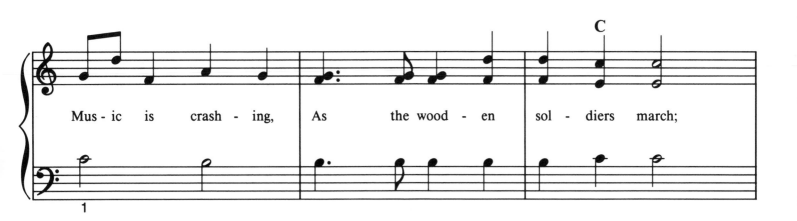

Mus - ic is crash - ing, As the wood - en sol - diers march;

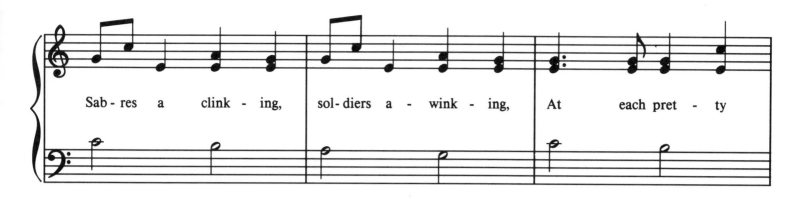

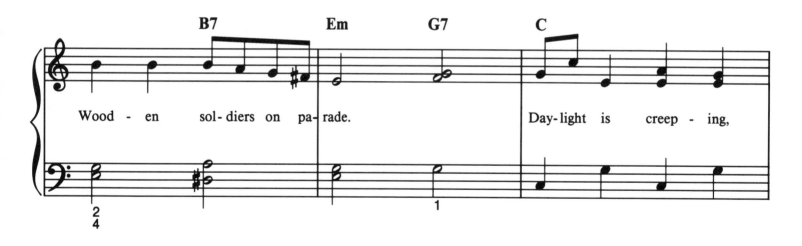

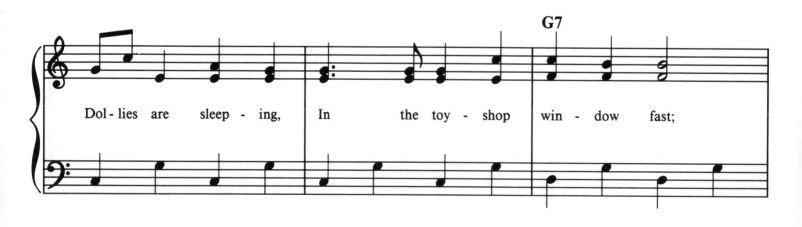

Sol-diers so jol-ly, Think of each dol-ly, Dream - ing of the

C

night that's past; When in the morn - ing, with-out a warn - ing,

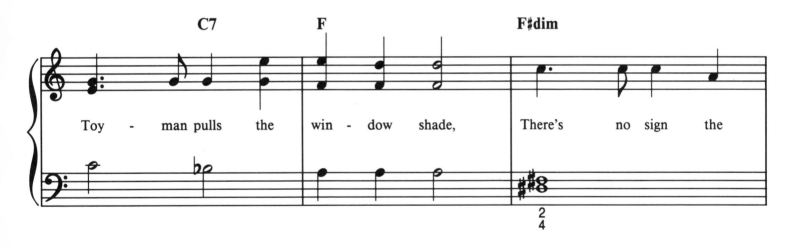

C7 **F** **F♯dim**

Toy - man pulls the win - dow shade, There's no sign the

$\frac{2}{4}$

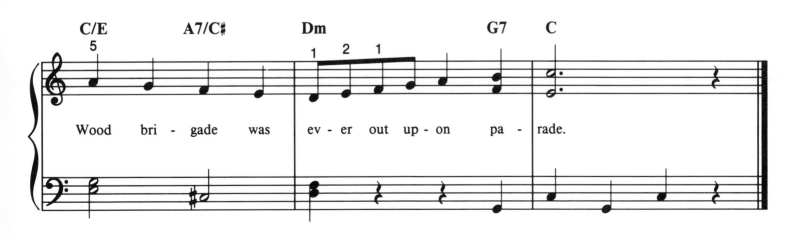

C/E **A7/C♯** **Dm** **G7** **C**

Wood bri - gade was ev - er out up-on pa - rade.

ROCKIN' AROUND THE CHRISTMAS TREE

Music and Lyrics by
JOHNNY MARKS

209

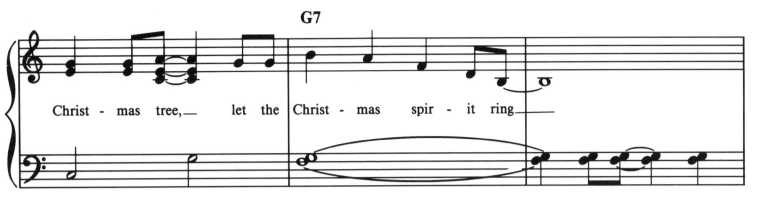

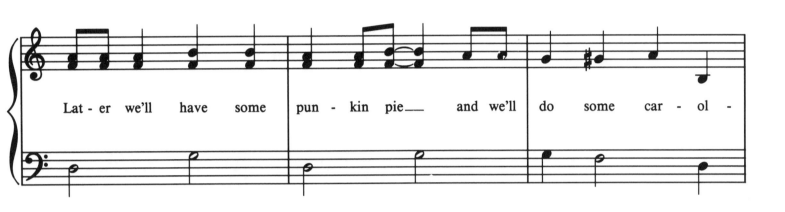

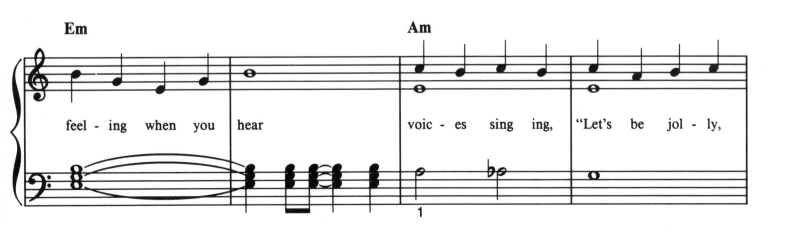

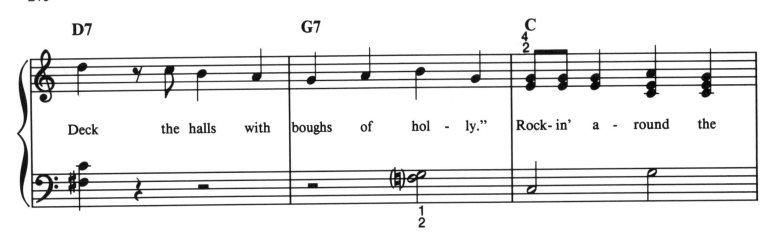

Deck the halls with boughs of hol - ly." Rock-in' a - round the

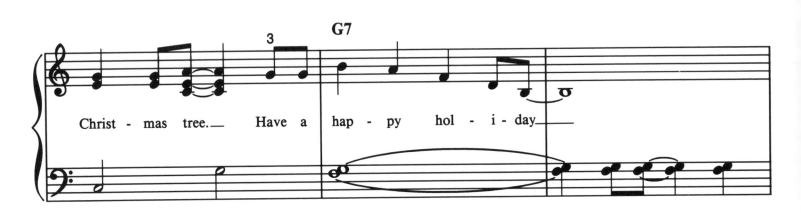

Christ - mas tree.___ Have a hap - py hol - i - day___

Ev- 'ry- one danc - ing mer - ri - ly___ in the new old fash - ioned

way.

RUDOLPH THE RED-NOSED REINDEER

Music and Lyrics by
JOHNNY MARKS

212

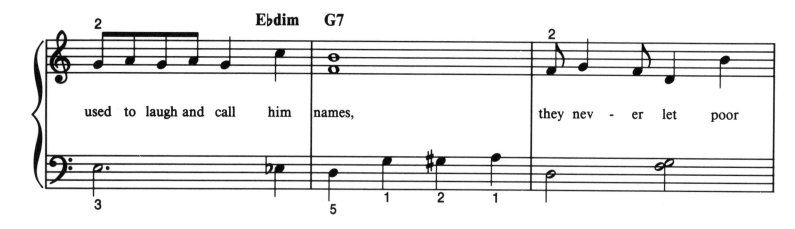

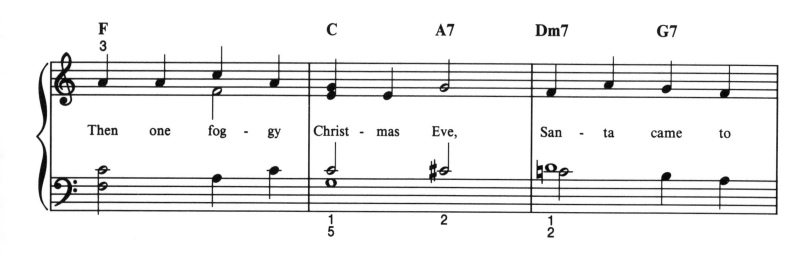

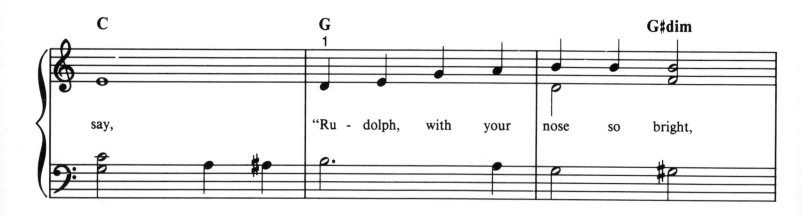

213

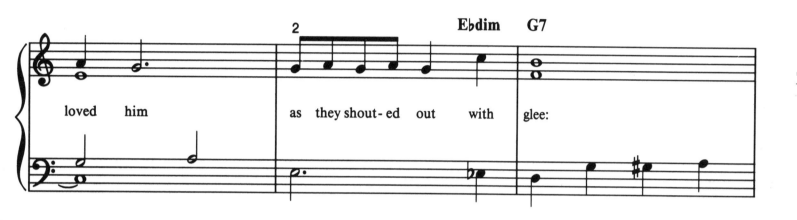

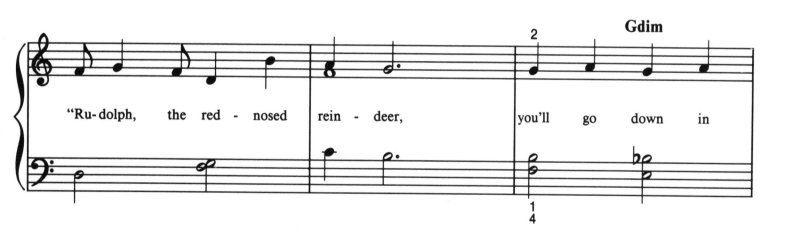

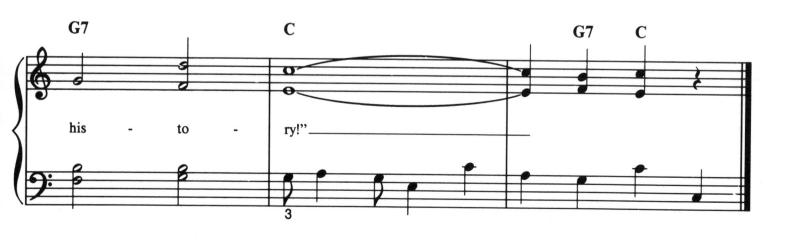

SANTA, BRING MY BABY BACK
(To Me)

Words and Music by CLAUDE DeMETRUIS
and AARON SCHROEDER

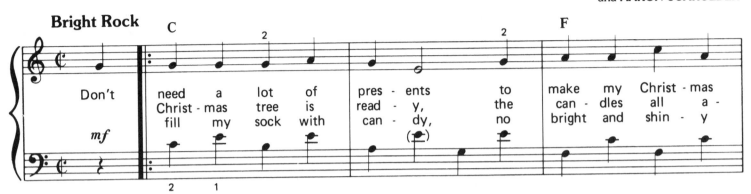

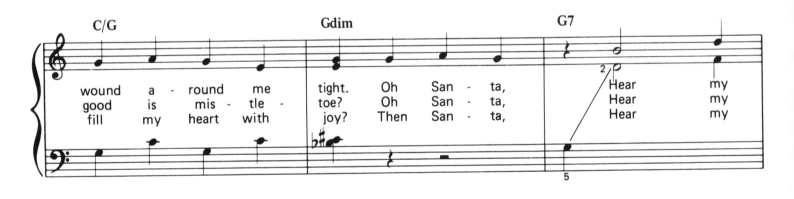

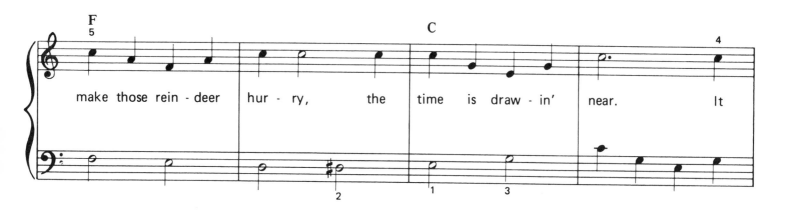

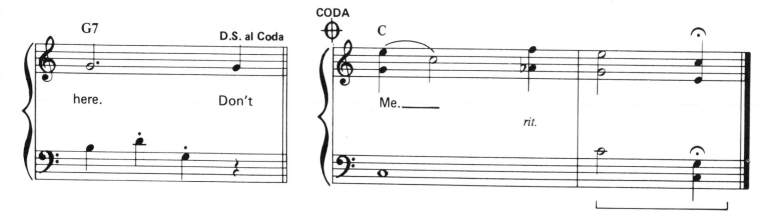

SHAKE ME I RATTLE
(Squeeze Me I Cry)

Words and Music by HAL HACKADY
and CHARLES NAYLOR

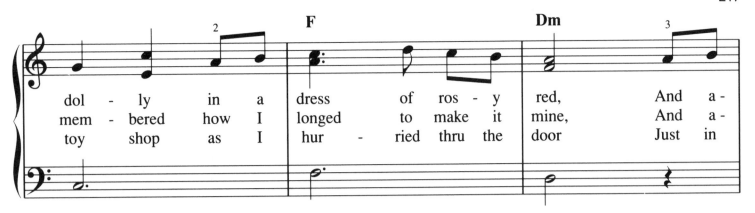

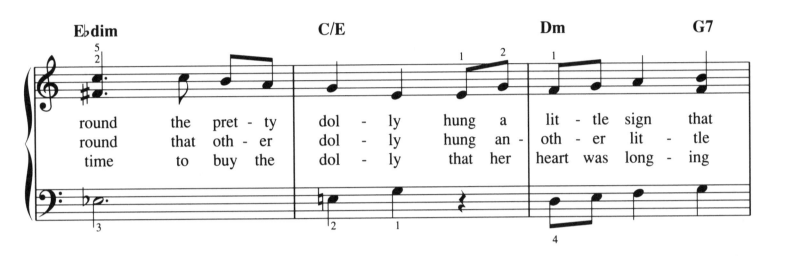

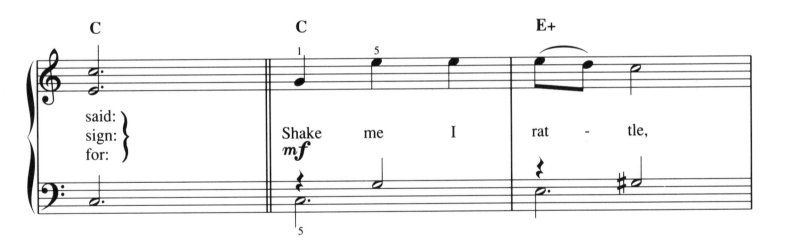

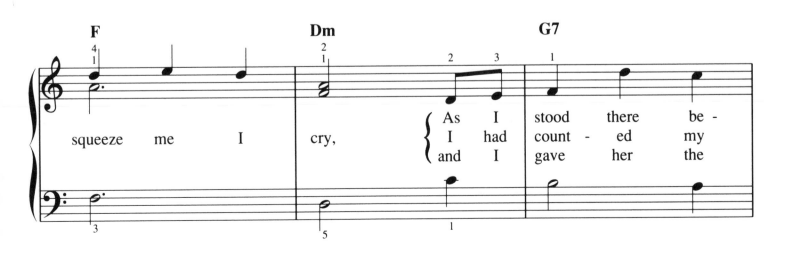

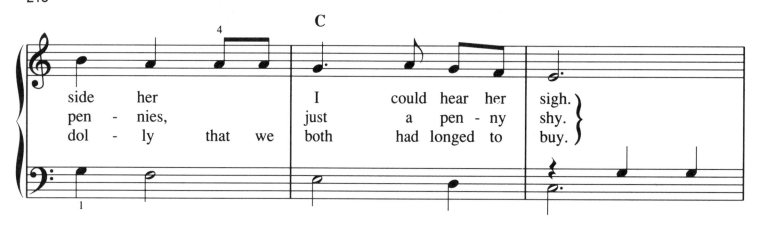

side her   I   could hear her   sigh.
pen - nies,   just   a   pen - ny   shy.
dol - ly   that   we   both   had longed to   buy.

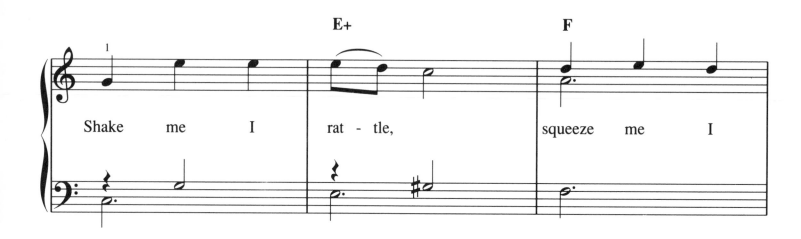

Shake me   I   rat - tle,   squeeze me   I

cry,   Please   take   me   home   and

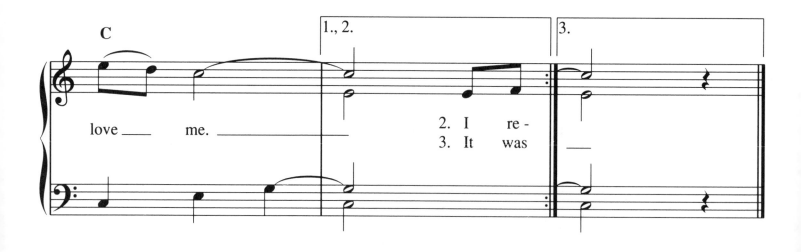

love ____ me. ____   2. I re -
                                        3. It was

SILVER AND GOLD

Music and Lyrics by
JOHNNY MARKS

220

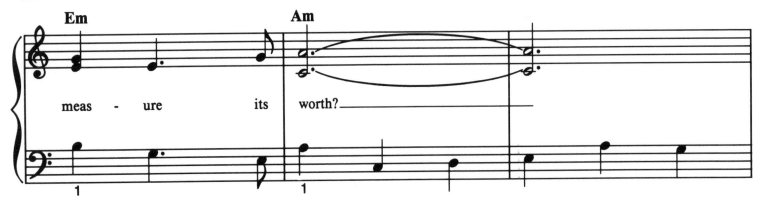

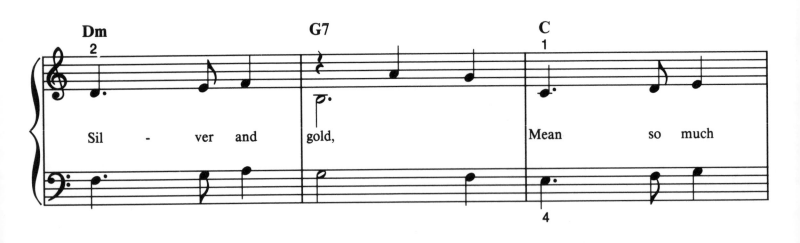

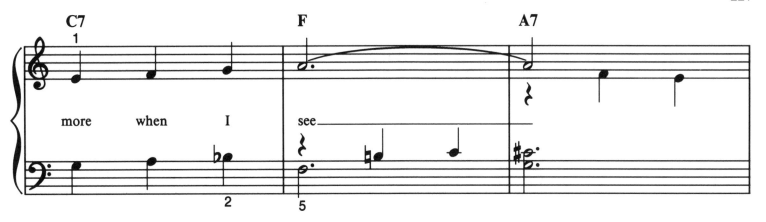

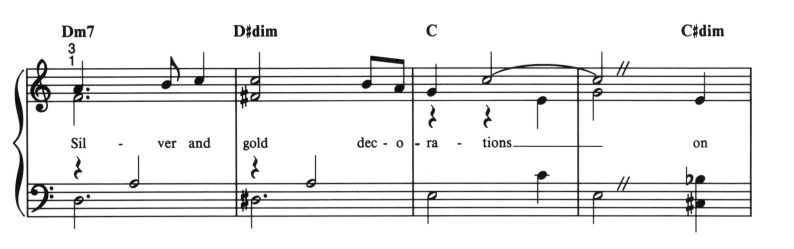

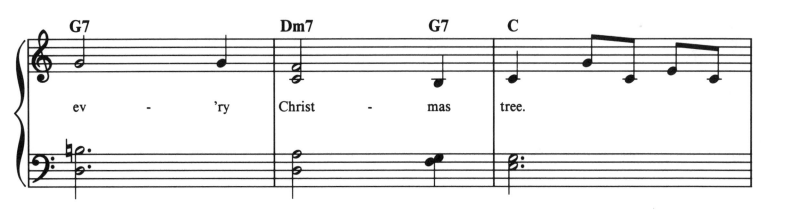

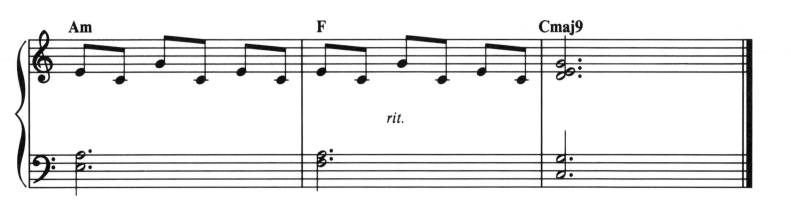

SILENT NIGHT

Words by JOSEPH MOHR
Translated by JOHN F. YOUNG
Music by FRANZ X. GRUBER

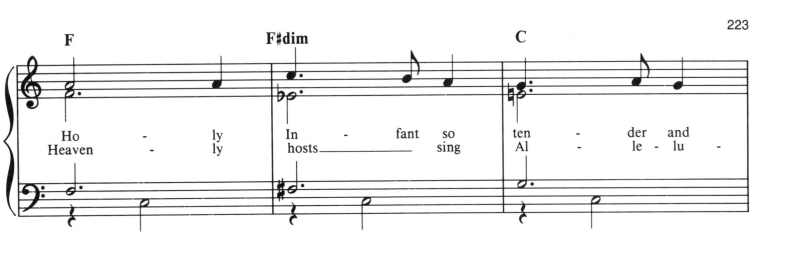

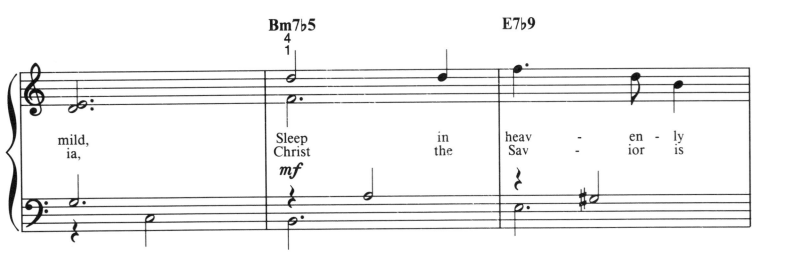

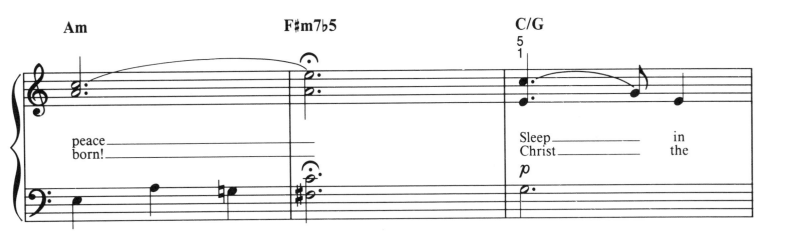

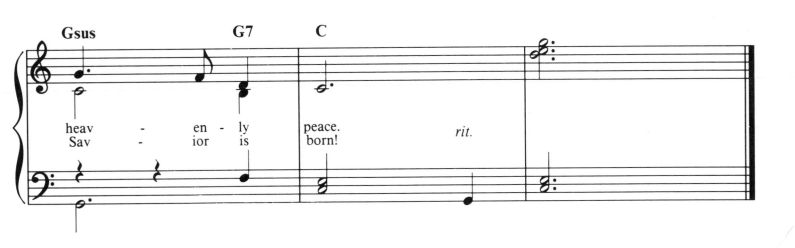

SILVER BELLS
from the Paramount Picture THE LEMON DROP KID

Words and Music by JAY LIVINGSTON
and RAY EVANS

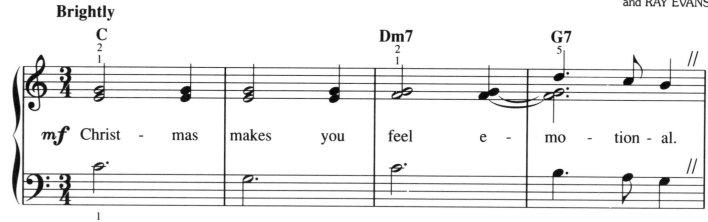

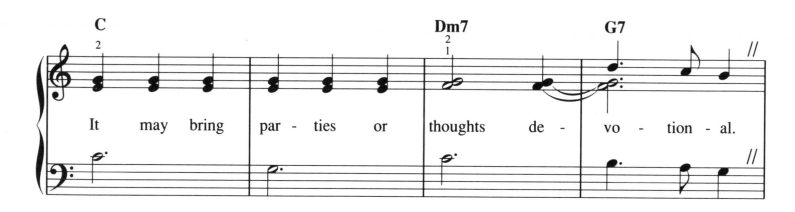

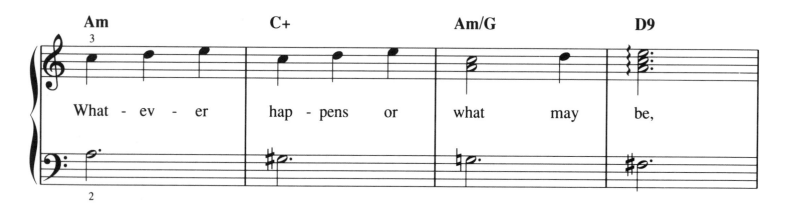

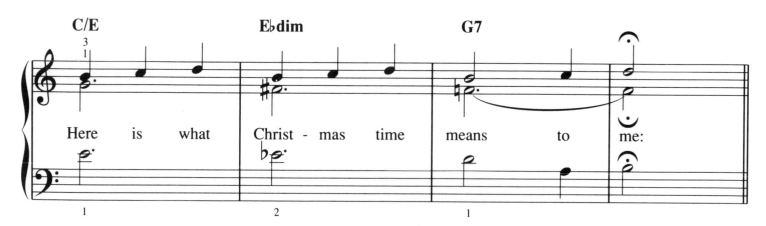

225

Chorus
Moderately

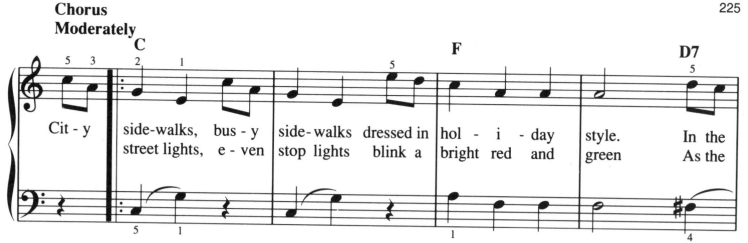

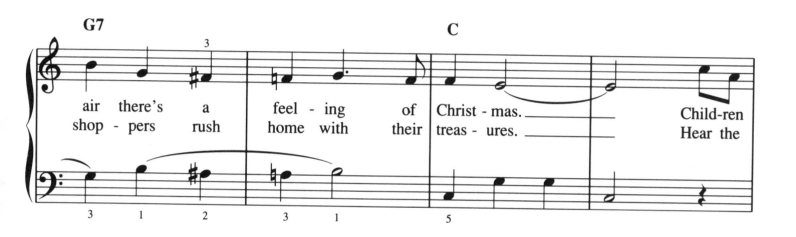

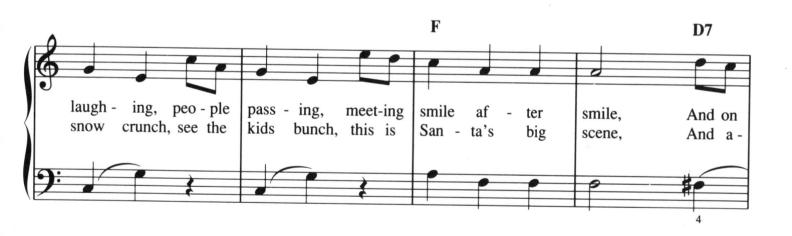

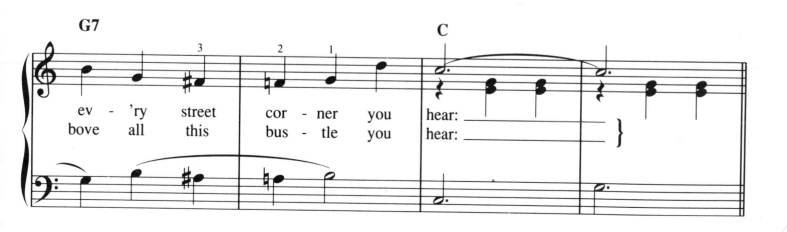

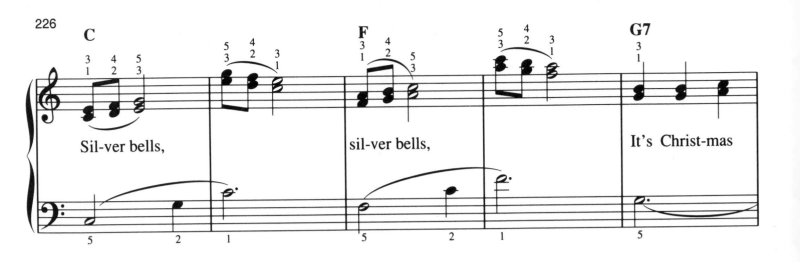

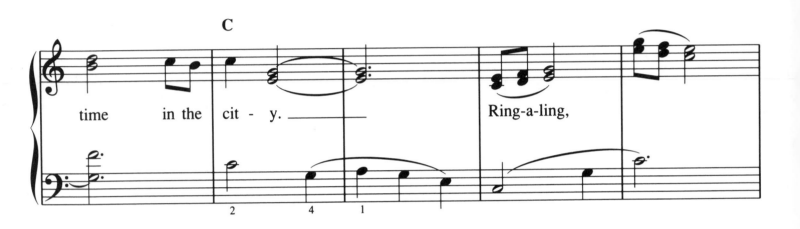

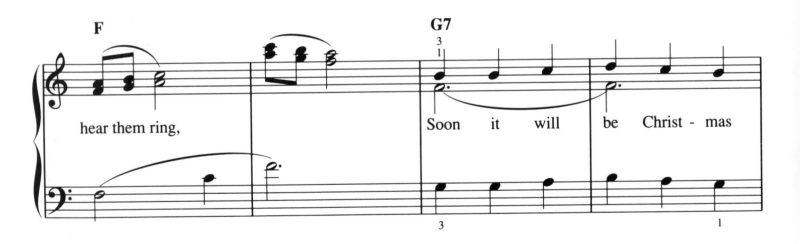

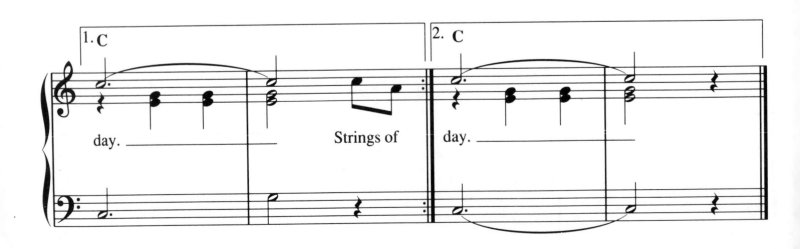

WHEN SANTA CLAUS GETS YOUR LETTER

Music and Lyrics by
JOHNNY MARKS

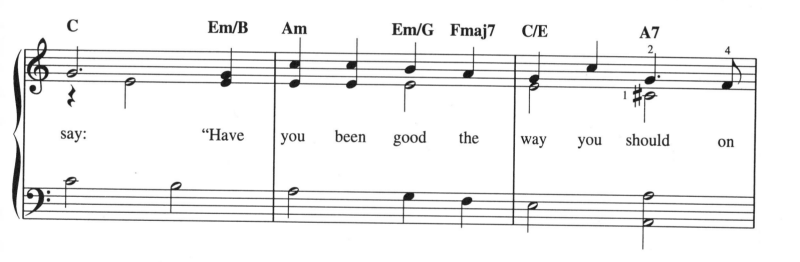

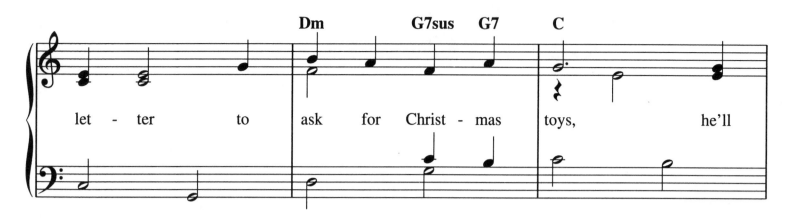

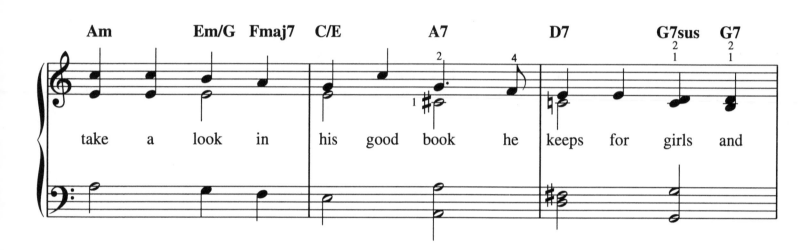

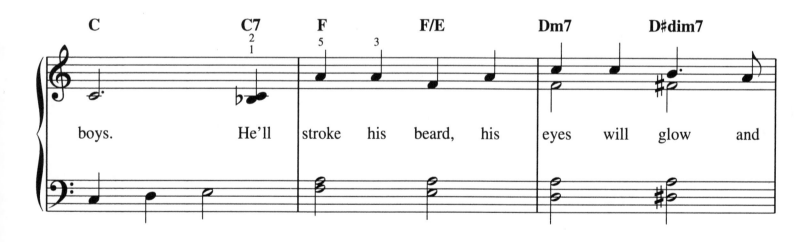

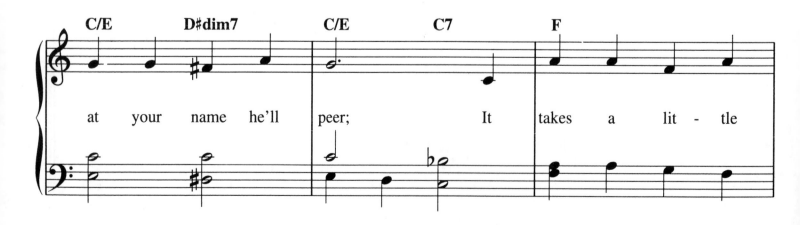

SLEEP, HOLY BABE

Words by EDWARD CASWELL
Music by J.B. DYKES

Sleep, Ho - ly Babe, Thine an - gels _ watch a-

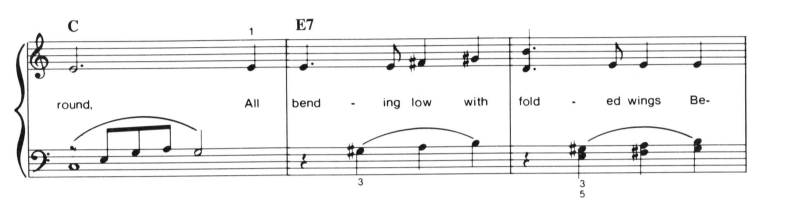

round, All bend - ing low with fold - ed wings Be-

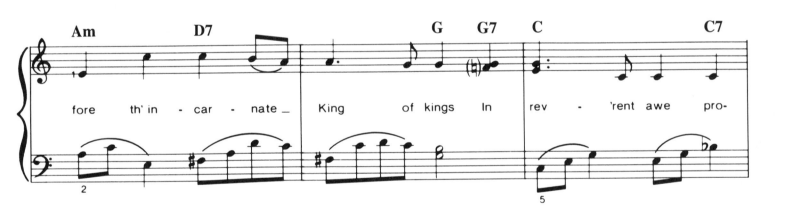

fore th'in - car - nate _ King of kings In rev - 'rent awe pro-

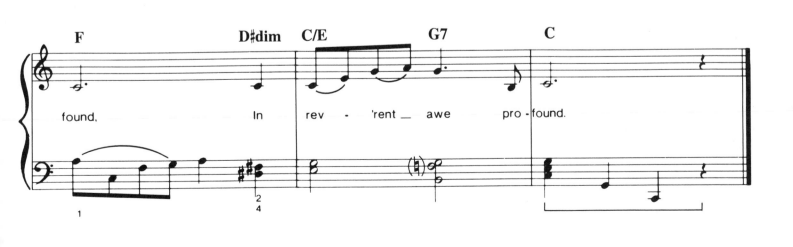

found, In rev - 'rent _ awe pro - found.

SOME CHILDREN SEE HIM

Lyric by WIHLA HUTSON
Music by ALFRED BURT

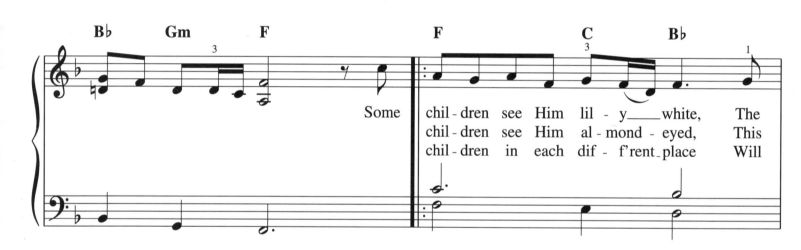

Some chil - dren see Him lil - y __ white, The
chil - dren see Him al - mond - eyed, This
chil - dren in each dif - f'rent place Will

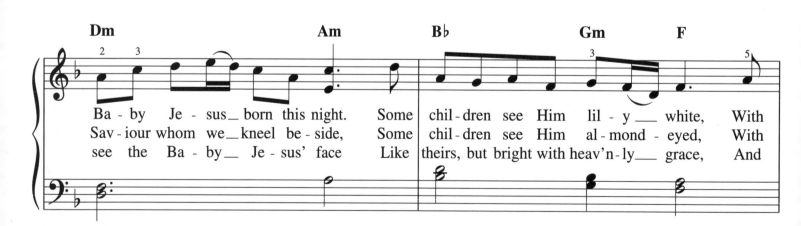

Ba - by Je - sus __ born this night. Some chil - dren see Him lil - y __ white, With
Sav - iour whom we __ kneel be - side, Some chil - dren see Him al - mond - eyed, With
see the Ba - by __ Je - sus' face Like theirs, but bright with heav'n - ly __ grace, And

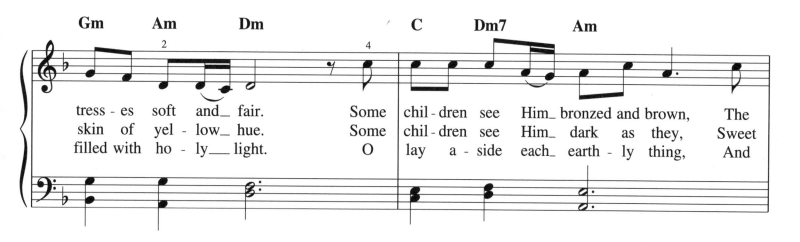

tress - es soft and_ fair. Some chil-dren see Him_ bronzed and brown, The
skin of yel - low_ hue. Some chil-dren see Him dark as they, Sweet
filled with ho - ly_ light. O lay a - side each_ earth - ly thing, And

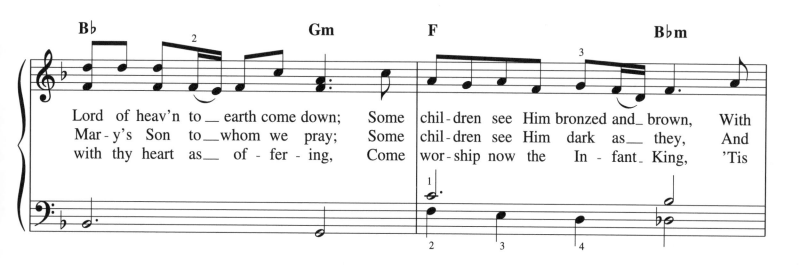

Lord of heav'n to _ earth come down; Some chil-dren see Him bronzed and_ brown, With
Mar - y's Son to_whom we pray; Some chil-dren see Him dark as_ they, And
with thy heart as_ of - fer - ing, Come wor-ship now the In - fant_ King, 'Tis

1.,2.
dark and heav - y ___ hair. Some
ah! they love him_ too! The

3.
love that's born to - night!

THE STAR CAROL

Lyric by WIHLA HUTSON
Music by ALFRED BURT

Tenderly, with much expression

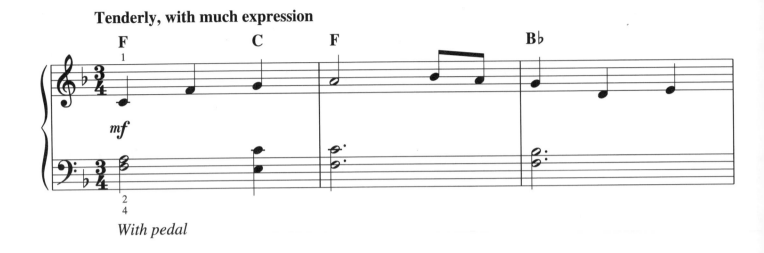

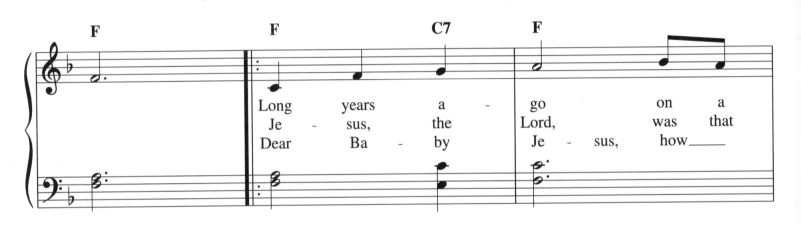

Long years a - go on a
Je - sus, the Lord, was that
Dear Ba - by Je - sus, how

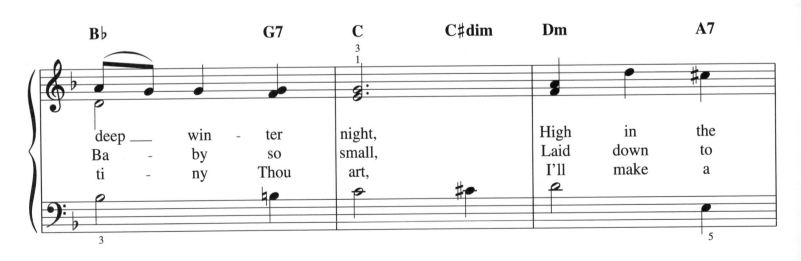

deep win - ter night,
Ba - by so small,
ti - ny Thou art,

High in the
Laid down to
I'll make a

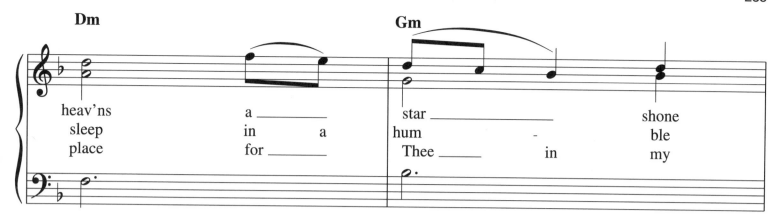

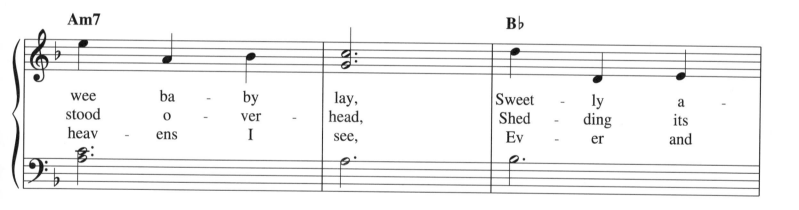

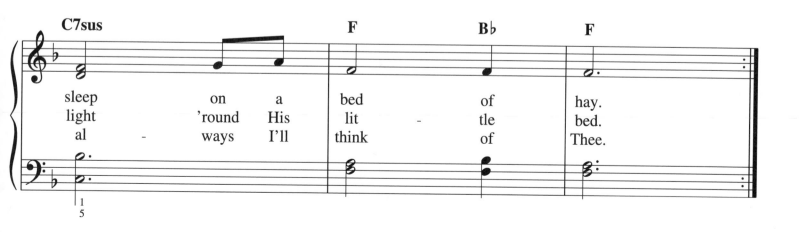

STILL, STILL, STILL

Salzburg Melody, c.1819
Traditional Austrian Text

SUZY SNOWFLAKE

Words and Music by SID TEPPER
and ROY BENNETT

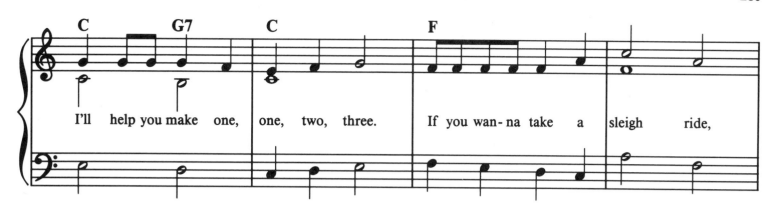

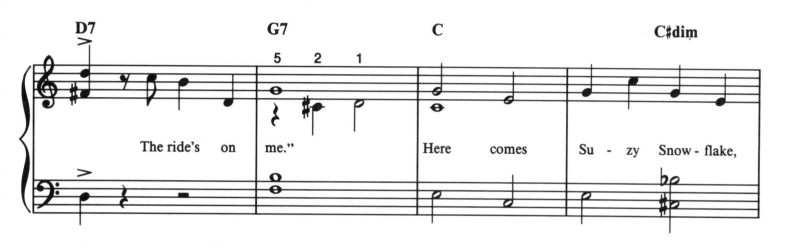

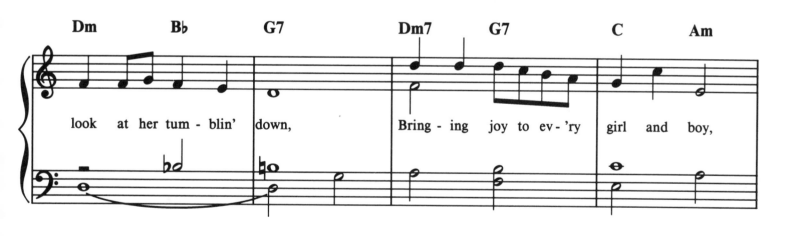

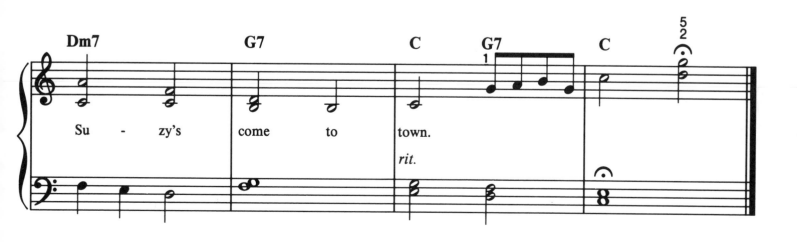

THAT CHRISTMAS FEELING

Words and Music by BENNIE BENJAMIN
and GEORGE WEISS

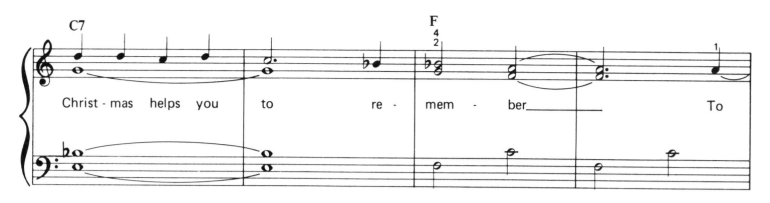

Christ - mas helps you to re - mem - ber_____ To

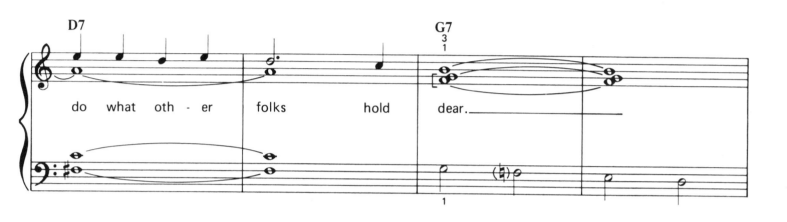

do what oth - er folks hold dear._____

What a bless - ed place the world would be if we

rall. - - - - - - - -

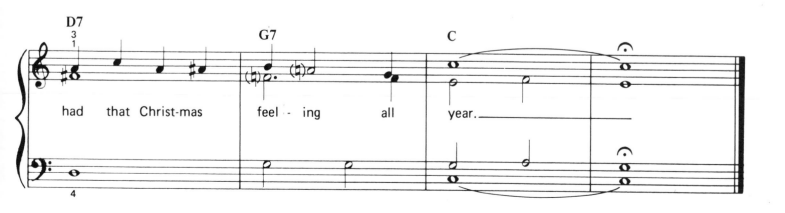

had that Christ - mas feel - ing all year._____

TOYLAND

Words by GLEN MacDONOUGH
Music by VICTOR HERBERT

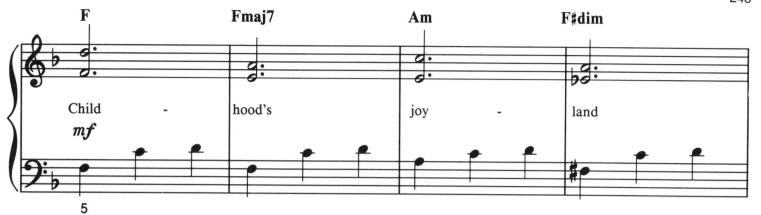

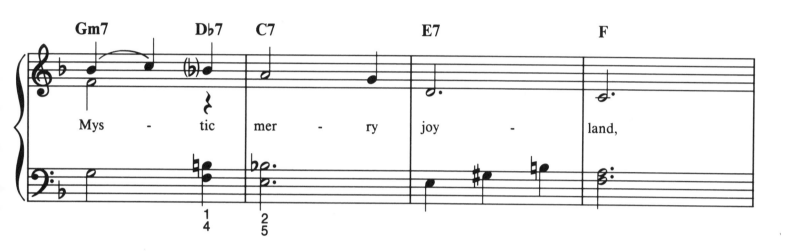

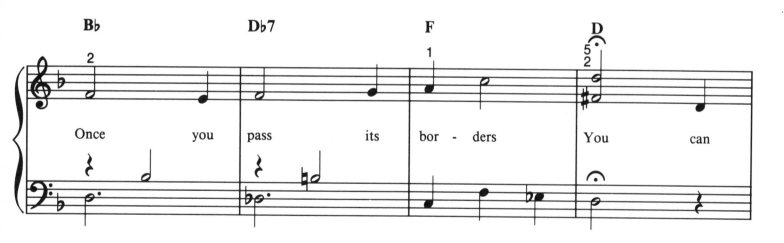

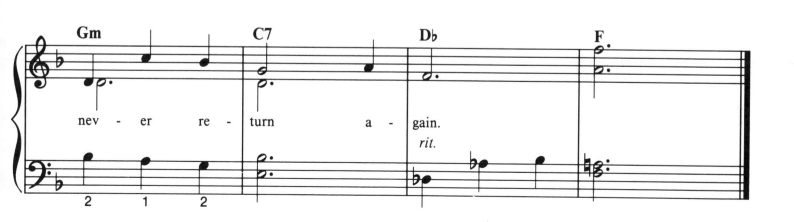

THE TWELVE DAYS OF CHRISTMAS

Traditional English Carol

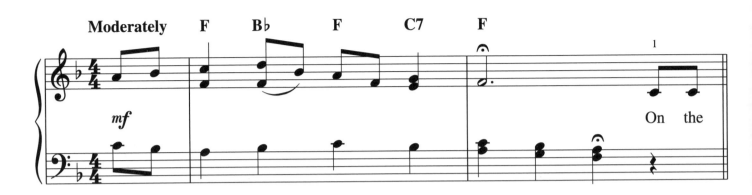

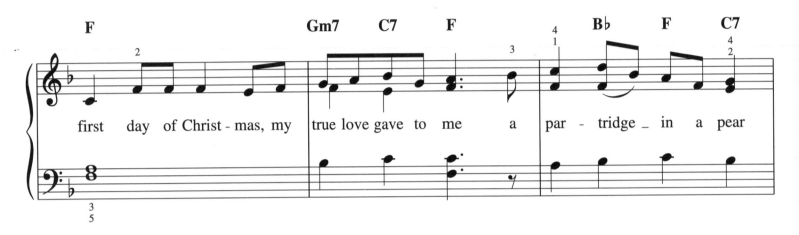

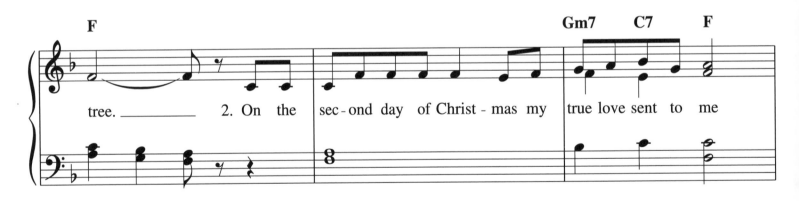

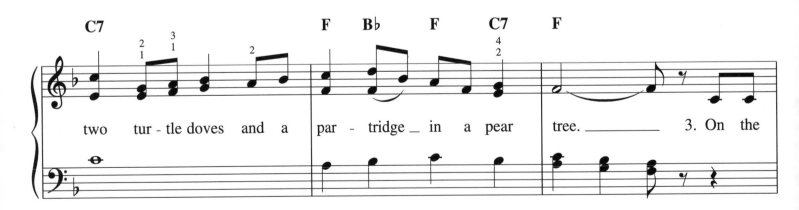

245

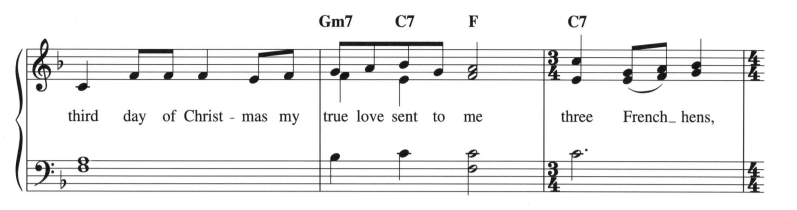

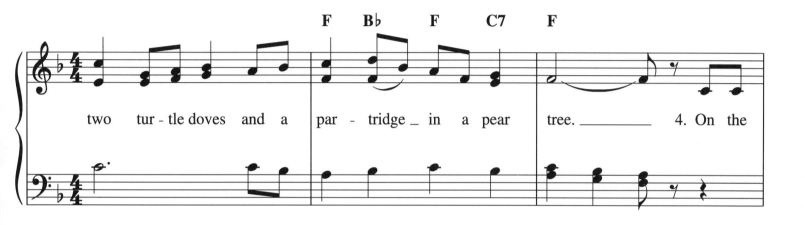

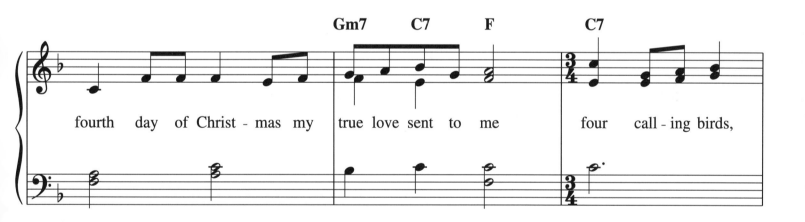

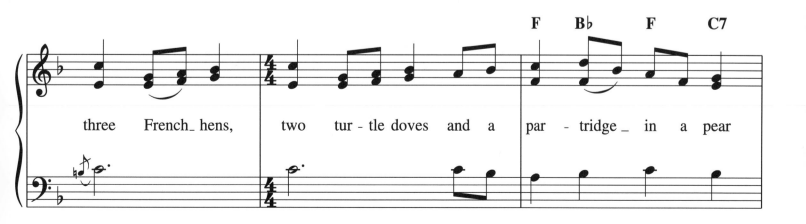

tree. _____ 5. On the fifth day of Christ-mas my true love sent to me

Slow and broad

Tempo Primo

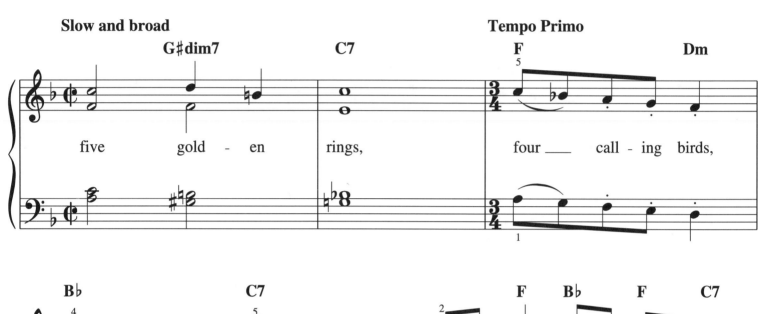

five gold - en rings, four ___ call - ing birds,

three French hens, two ___ tur - tle doves and a par - tridge ___ in a pear

tree. _____ 6. On the sixth day of Christ-mas my true love sent to me
7.-12. *(See additional verses)*

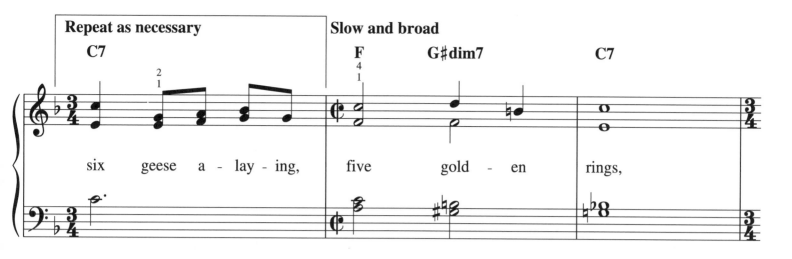

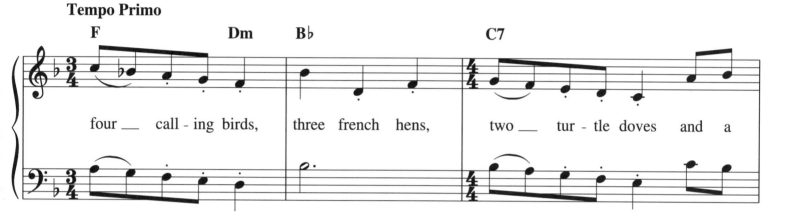

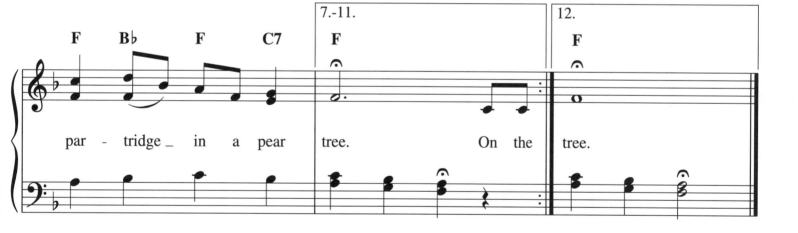

Additional Verses

Seven swans a-swimming
Eight maids a-milking
Nine ladies dancing
Ten lords a-leaping
Eleven pipers piping
Twelve drummers drumming

UP ON THE HOUSETOP

Words and Music by
B.R. HANDY

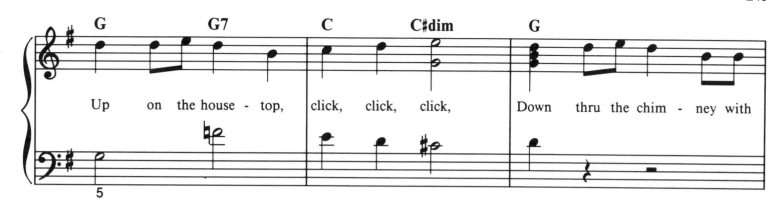

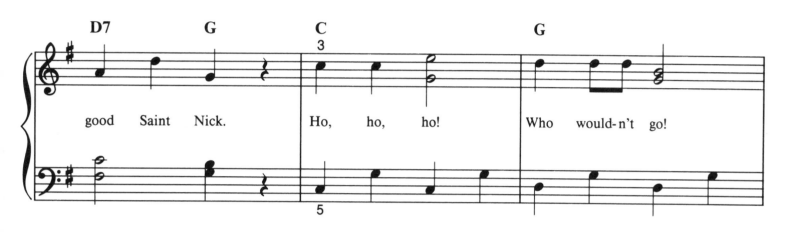

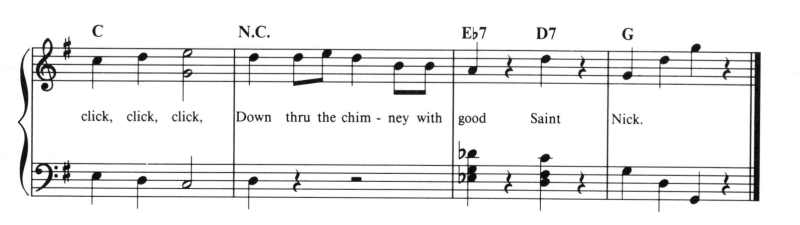

WE THREE KINGS OF ORIENT ARE

Words and Music by
JOHN H. HOPKINS, JR.

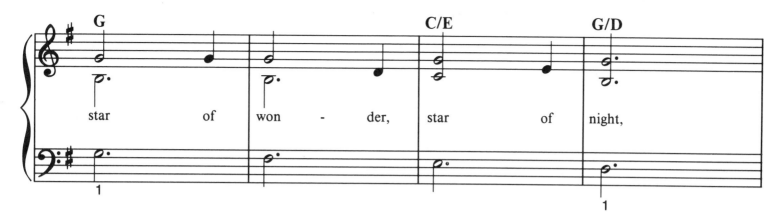

star of won - der, star of night,

Star with roy - al beau - ty bright,

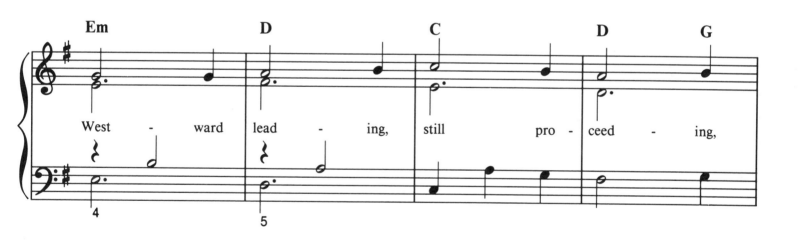

West - ward lead - ing, still pro - ceed - ing,

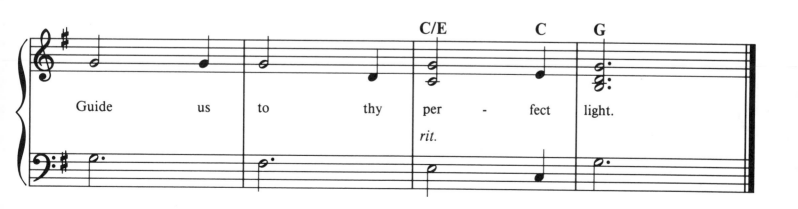

Guide us to thy per - fect light.

rit.

WE WISH YOU A MERRY CHRISTMAS

Traditional English Folksong

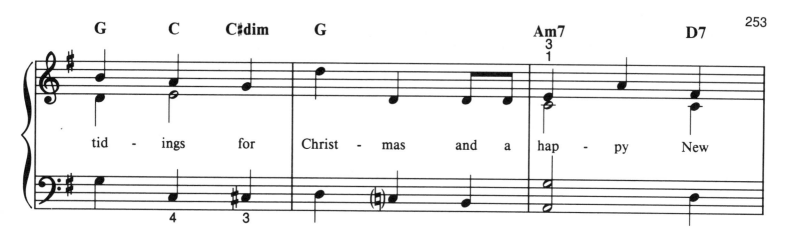

G   C   C#dim   G   Am7   D7   253

tid - ings   for   Christ - mas   and   a   hap - py   New

G   1   C

Year.   We   all   know   that   San - ta's   com - ing,   We
                   We   wish   you   a   mer - ry   Christ - mas,   We

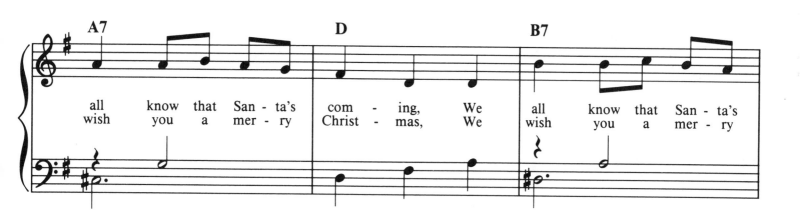

A7   D   B7

all   know   that   San - ta's   com - ing,   We   all   know   that   San - ta's
wish   you   a   mer - ry   Christ - mas,   We   wish   you   a   mer - ry

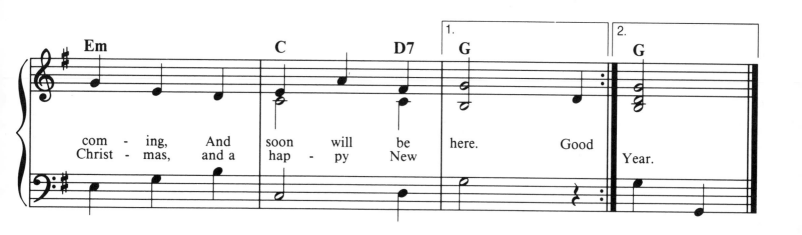

Em   C   D7   1. G   2. G

com - ing,   And   soon   will   be   here.   Good   Year.
Christ - mas,   and a   hap - py   be   New

WHAT CHILD IS THIS?

Words by WILLIAM C. DIX
16th Century English Melody

What Child is this, who, laid to rest, On
So bring Him in - cense, gold and myrrh, Come
Mar - y's lap is sleep - ing? Whom
peas - ant king to own Him;
an - gels greet with an - thems sweet, While
King of kings sal - va - tion brings, Let
shep - herds watch are keep - ing?
lov - ing hearts en - throne Him.

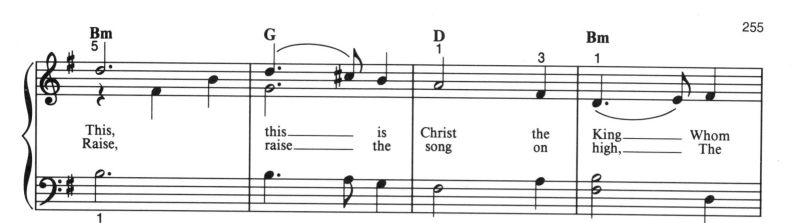

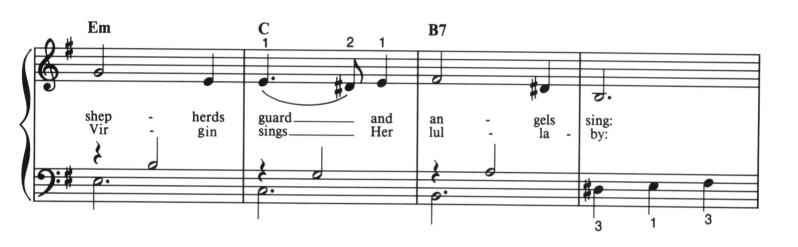

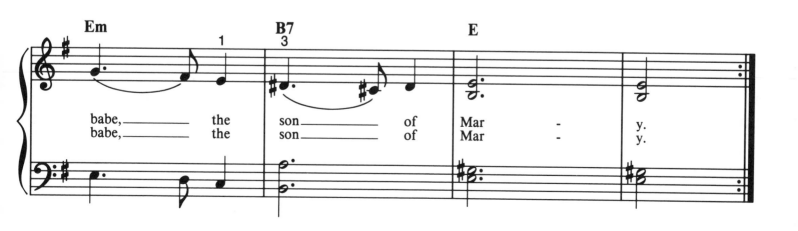

WHILE SHEPHERDS WATCHED THEIR FLOCKS

Words by NAHUM TATE
Music by GEORGE FRIDERIC HANDEL

THE WHITE WORLD OF WINTER

Words by MITCHELL PARISH
Music by HOAGY CARMICHAEL

Moderately, with a lift

(L.H. over)

In this / won - der - ful white world of win - ter, ___

won - der - ful white world of win - ter, ___

dar - ling, we'll have a won - der - ful time. ___

dar - ling, we'll have a won - der - ful time. ___

First, we'll ride side by side thru the hin - ter

If we prayed it would snow all this win - ter ___

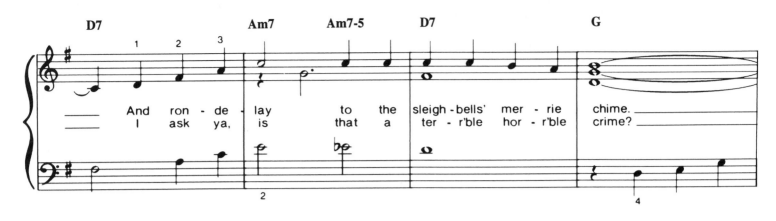

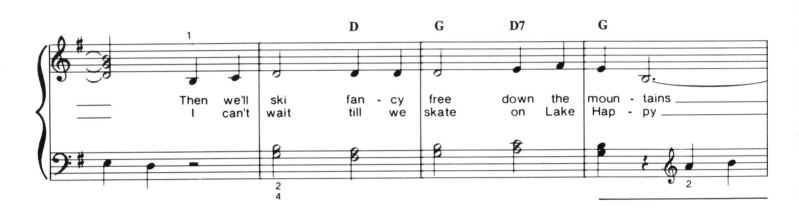

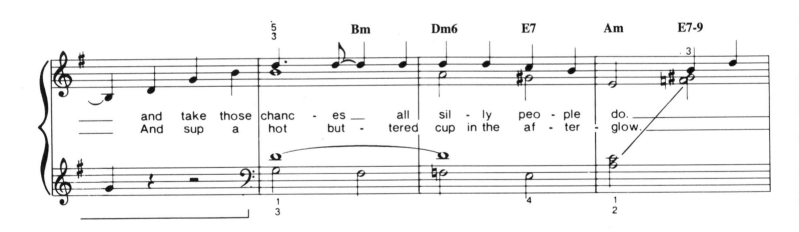

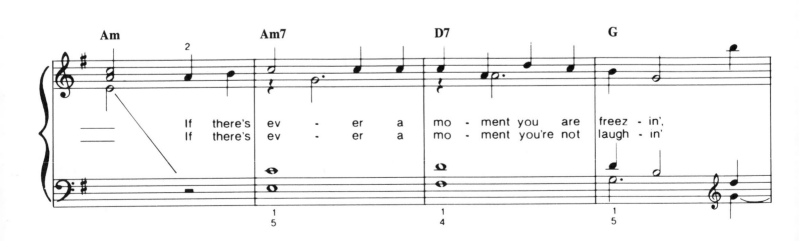

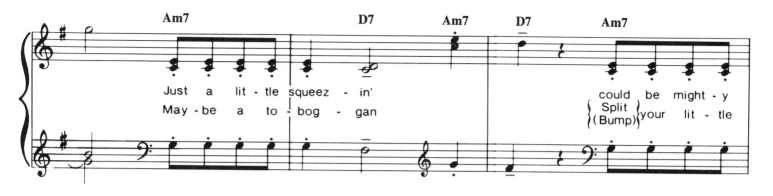

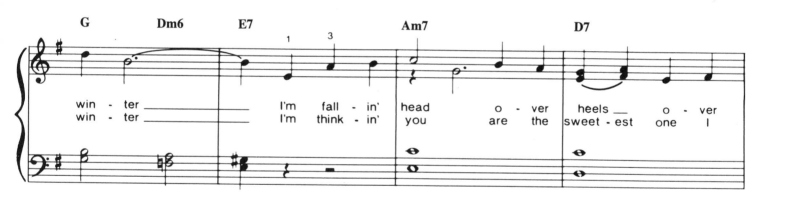

259

WHO WOULD IMAGINE A KING

from the Touchstone Motion Picture THE PREACHER'S WIFE

Words and Music by MERVYN WARREN
and HALLERIN HILTON HILL

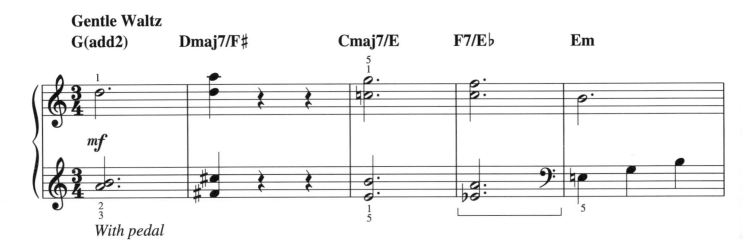

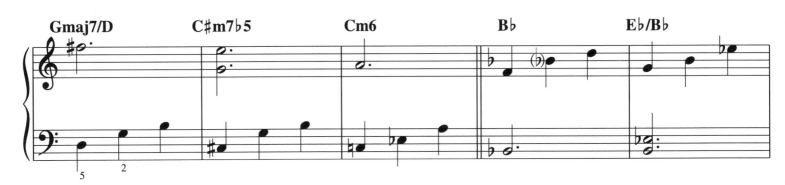

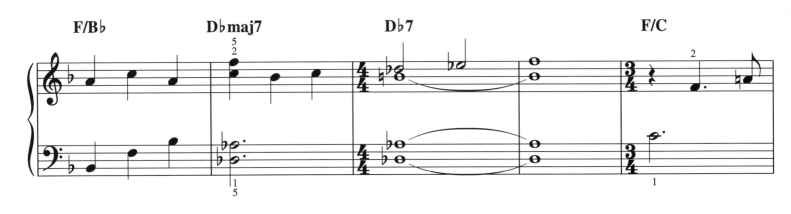

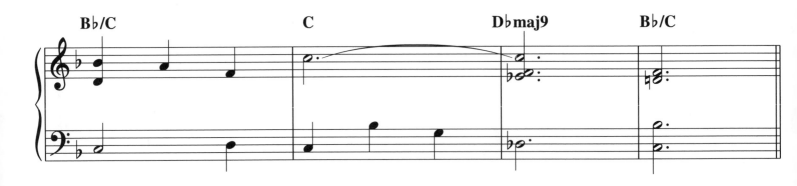

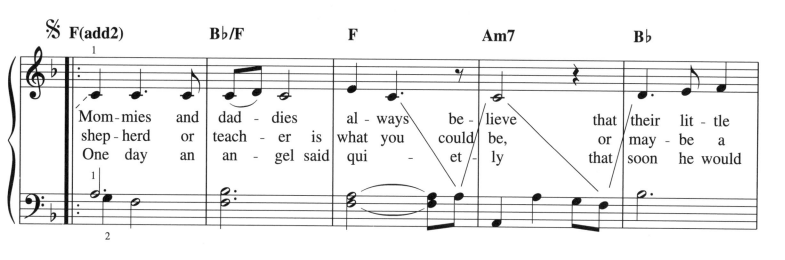

%& **F(add2)**   **Bb/F**   **F**   **Am7**   **Bb**

Mom - mies and dad - dies al - ways be - lieve that their lit - tle
shep - herd or teach - er is what you could be, or may - be a
One day an an - gel said qui - et - ly that soon he would

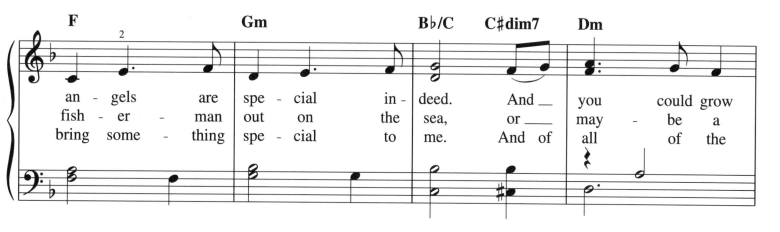

F   **Gm**   **Bb/C**   **C#dim7**   **Dm**

an - gels are spe - cial in - deed. And __ you could grow
fish - er - man out on the sea, or __ may - be a
bring some - thing spe - cial to me. And of all of the

To Coda ⊕

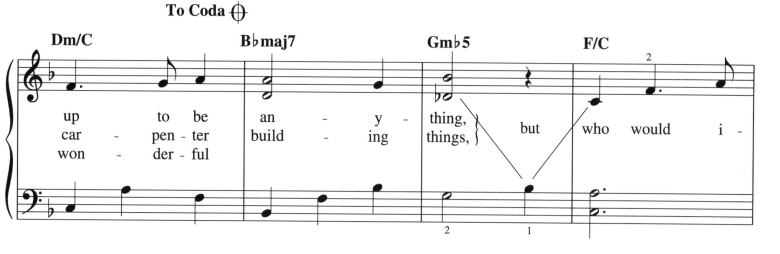

Dm/C   **Bbmaj7**   **Gmb5**   **F/C**

up to be an - y - thing,
car - pen - ter build - ing things, but who would i -
won - der - ful

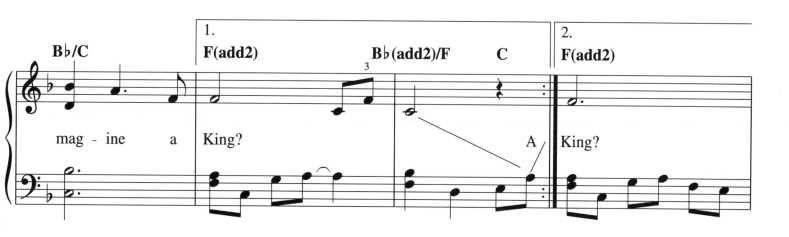

Bb/C | 1.   **F(add2)**   **Bb(add2)/F**   **C** || 2.   **F(add2)**

mag - ine a King?   A King?

262

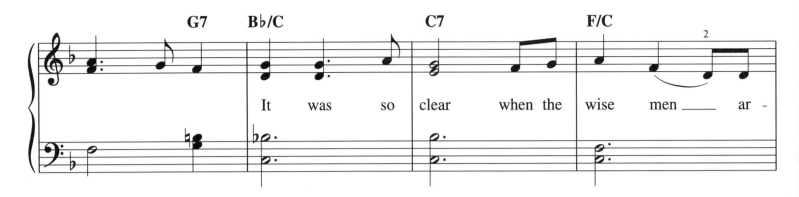

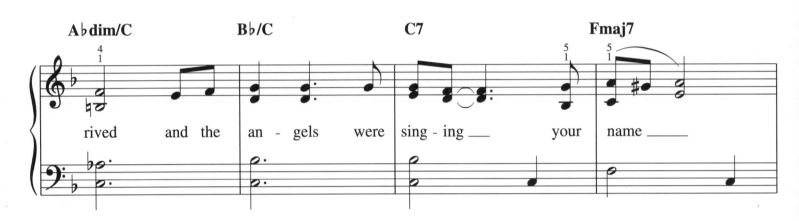

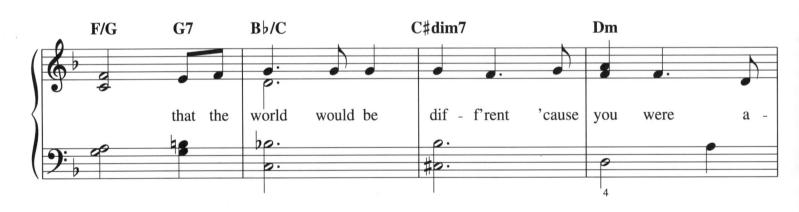

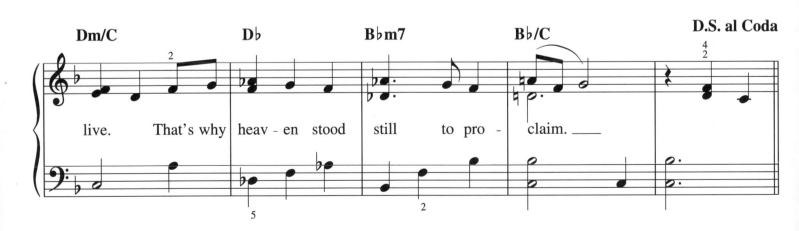

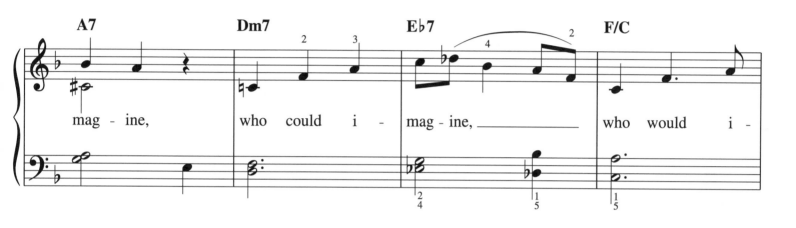

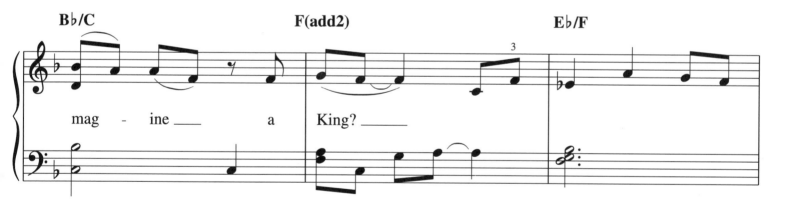

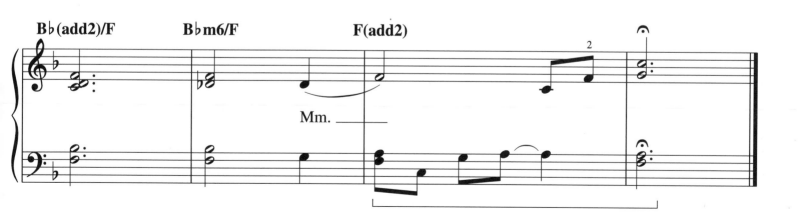

WONDERFUL CHRISTMASTIME

Words and Music by
McCARTNEY

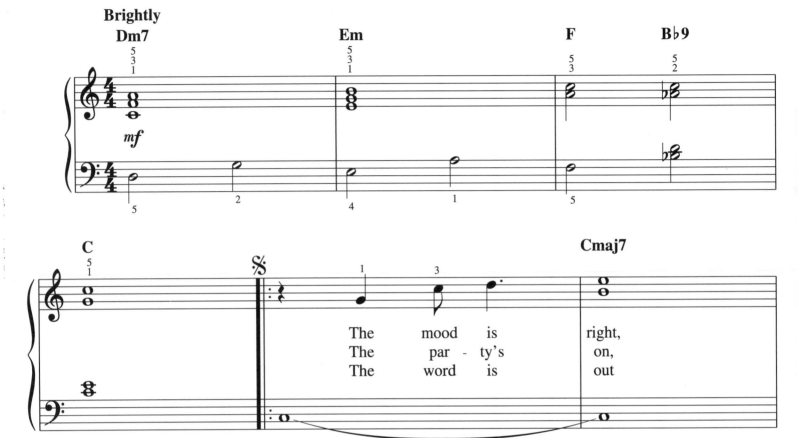

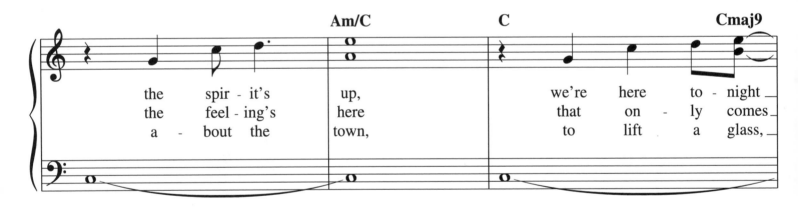

The mood is right,
The par - ty's on,
The word is out

the spir - it's up,
the feel - ing's here
a - bout the town,

we're here to - night
that on - ly comes
to lift a glass,

and that's e - nough.
this time of year.
oh don't look down.

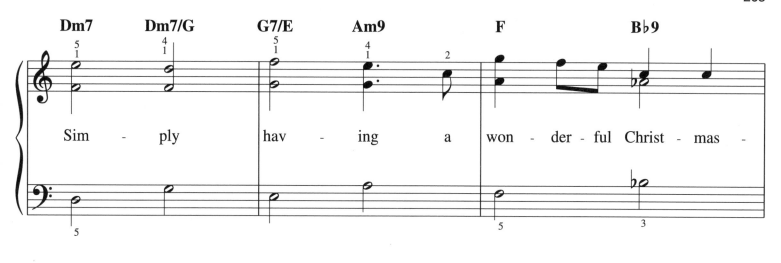

Sim - ply hav - ing a won - der - ful Christ - mas -

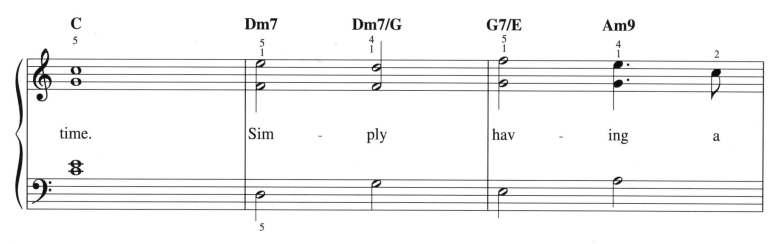

time. Sim - ply hav - ing a

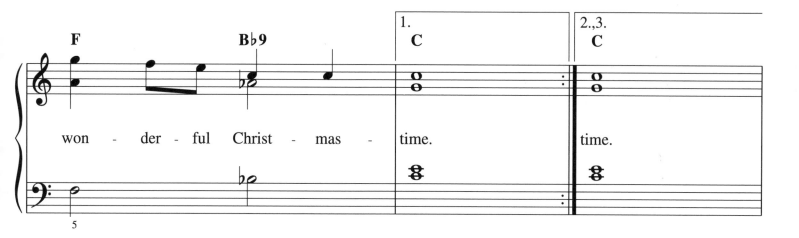

won - der - ful Christ - mas - time. time.

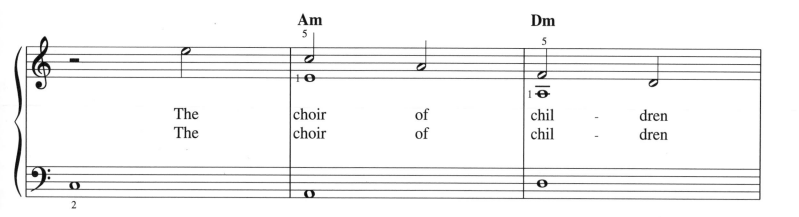

The choir of chil - dren
The choir of chil - dren

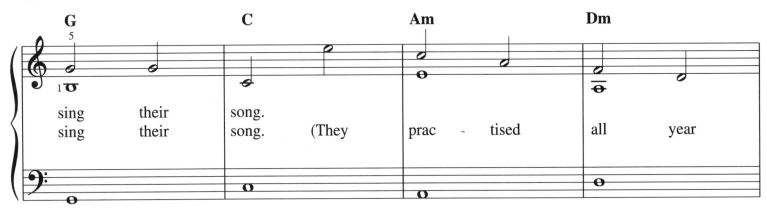

sing their song.
sing their song. (They prac - tised all year

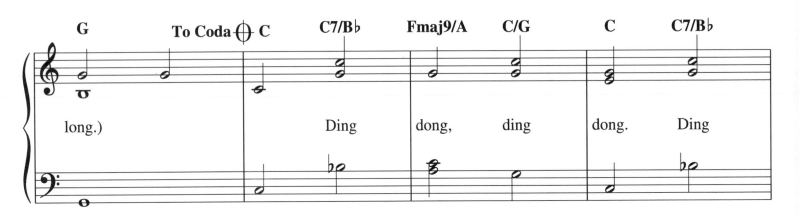

long.)
Ding dong, ding dong. Ding

dong, ding.
Ooh _____ Ooh. ____

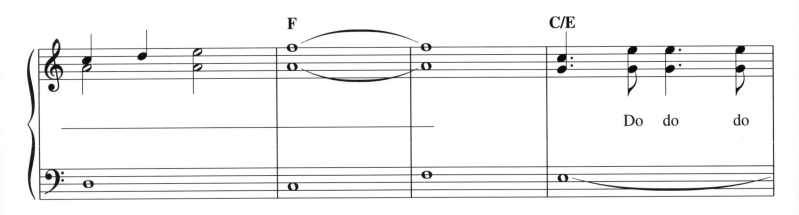

Do do do

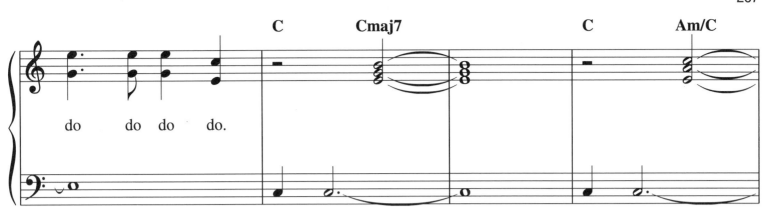

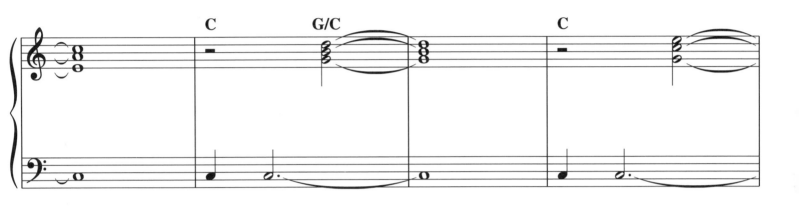

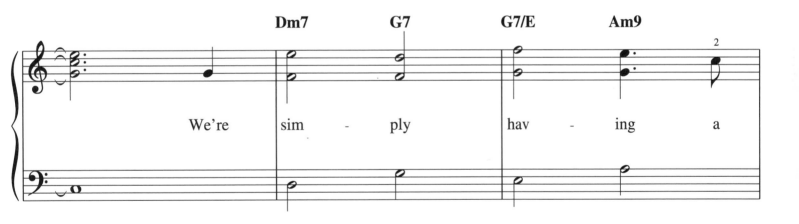

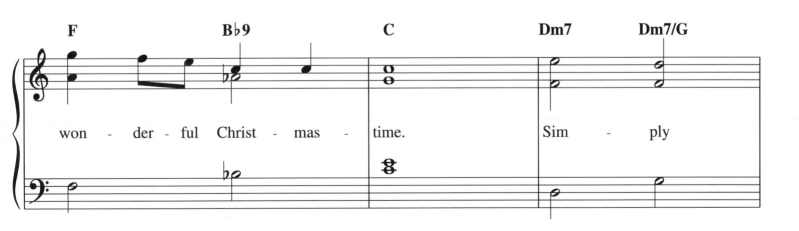

having a won-der-ful Christ-mas-time.

D.S. al Coda

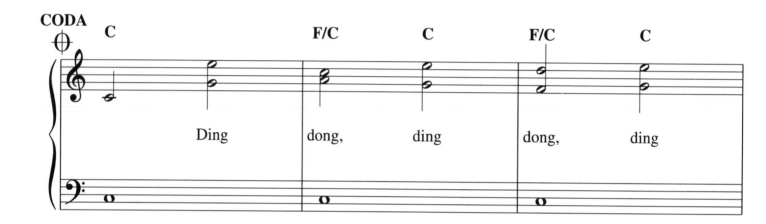

CODA

Ding dong, ding dong, ding

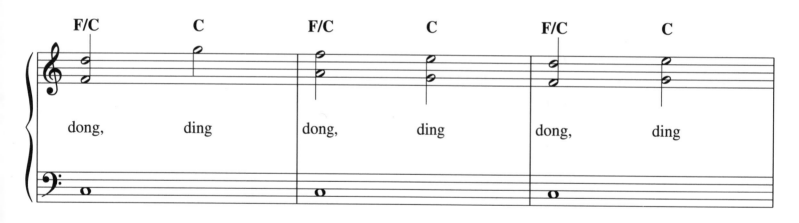

dong, ding dong, ding dong, ding

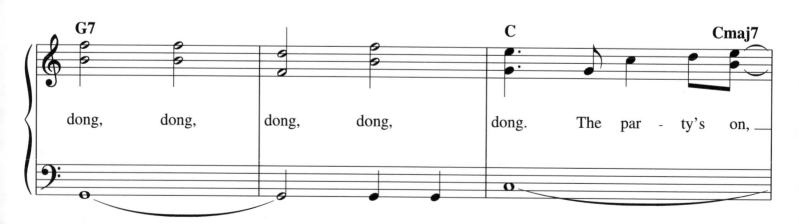

dong, dong, dong, dong, dong. The par-ty's on,

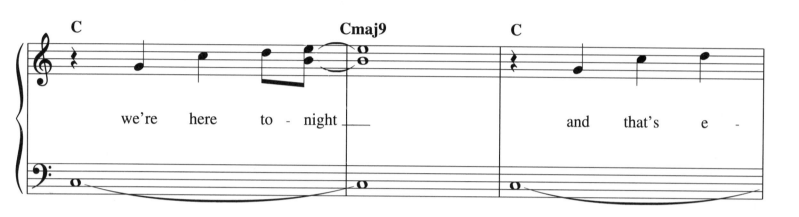

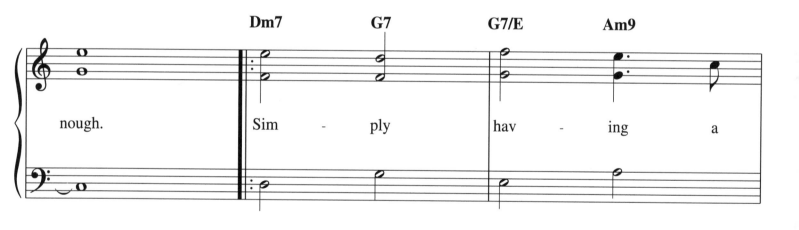

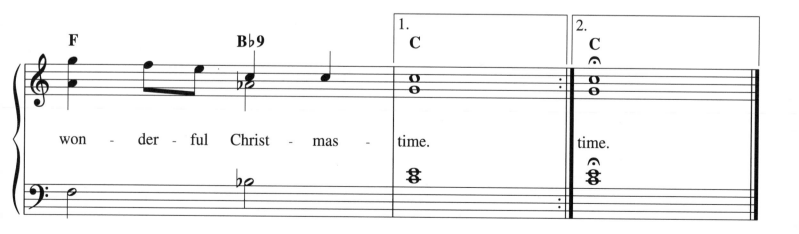

THE WONDERFUL WORLD OF CHRISTMAS

Words by CHARLES TOBIAS
Music by AL FRISCH

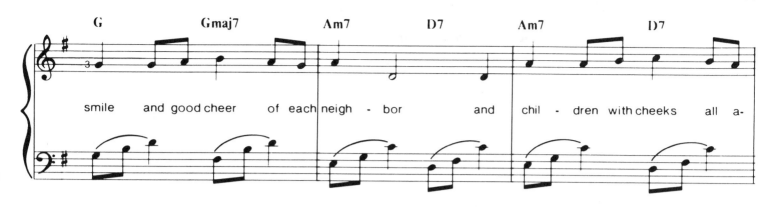

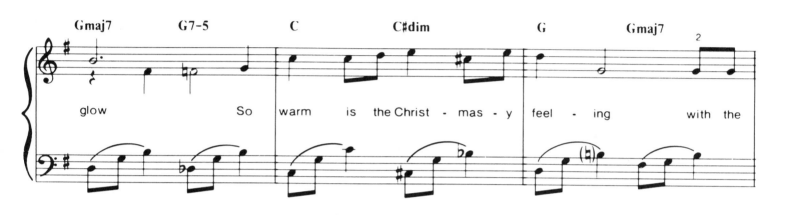

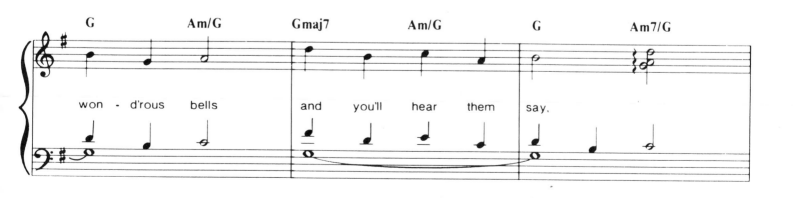

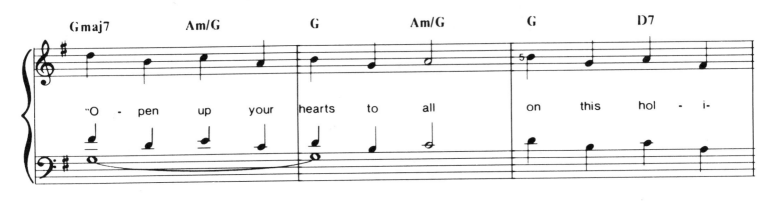

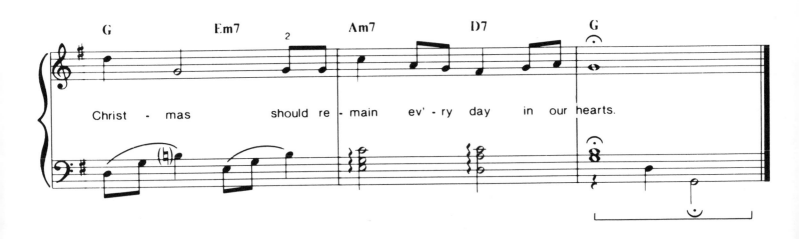